YOU'VE CHANGED

YOU'VE CHANGED

*Fake Accents, Feminism,
and Other Comedies
from Myanmar*

PYAE MOE THET WAR

Catapult   New York

This is a book of personal essays. It reflects the author's recollections of experiences over time. Some names and identifying details have been changed to protect the privacy of individuals.

ISBN: 978-1-64622-107-3

Jacket design by Jaya Miceli
Book design by Jordan Koluch

Library of Congress Control Number: 2021941006

Catapult
New York, NY
books.catapult.co

Printed in the United States of America
10 9 8 7 6 5 4 3 2 1

To Mommy,
who took me to all the libraries and bookshops,
who let me store whatever book I was currently reading in her
purse no matter how heavy it was, and who believed that I
could and would write my own book one day, way before I even
believed it myself. I love you so much.

Contents

YOU'VE CHANGED

A ME BY ANY OTHER NAME

have two names, which is one whole name more than most people have. I've been asked about it all my life. Usually I just smile and say, "It's a long story." My legal name—that is, the one on my birth certificate and passport and other bureaucratic documentation—is Moe Thet War, but everyone calls me Pyae Pyae (or Pyae, depending on how close we are). I guess technically the latter is a nickname, but it feels wrong to call it so. After all, my parents picked it out with as much careful consideration as they did Moe Thet War. Despite the number of times I've had this conversation, it's always a strange experience for me to explain the whole story to someone who doesn't get it. What's there to get (or not get)?

The first time I visited my boyfriend Toothpick's hometown in the East Midlands of jolly ol' England, his mother asked, "But which one is your christened Christian name? What were you given when you were baptized?" Even after multiple explanations, she and her

Catholic upbringing couldn't quite grasp that I didn't have a christened Christian name. My parents are Theravada Buddhists, which means we don't have baptisms, or any religious name-giving rites of a similar nature. In Myanmar culture, people believe that a good name will bring good karma for the rest of that person's life. My parents, especially my mom, are also highly religious and superstitious, so when I was born, they went to a palm reader whom they'd been seeing for years, like a family doctor. The palm reader then made the types of calculations that only palm readers know how to make, and she produced a list of names that would assure a bright and prosperous future for me (my literature and creative writing degrees would say that it didn't work).

My parents' only condition when they approached their all-knowing palm reader was that each of my potential names contain one of their names. They settled on Moe Thet War. I share the Moe from my dad's name, just as I share his patient temperament, and the Thet from my mom's, like I do her quiet but unyielding determination; I assume the War just worked out in the stars. Although I never use it except on official forms, I love this name because it feels like a concrete and constant reminder that, for better or for worse, my mom and dad are always a part of me.

Pyae Pyae was a separate yet seemingly equally complicated process, and it ties in with my siblings' names.

Pyae means "full." My brother's name, Phyo, means "grow," and my sister's name, Shan, means "overflow." My parents named us in this order so that, as an entity, we're first full of all the good things in life—wealth, health, happiness, love, et cetera—and then that number just keeps growing, until it's finally overflowing. Do I think it's a little over the top? Definitely, and I wonder how long they would've tried to keep this up if they'd had, say, eight children.

Like Pyae Pyae, the repetition of names is common in Myanmar culture; in addition to the example of my siblings, my grandmother, whom we call A May, is Myint Myint. In fact, all of my grandmother's sisters have names that are just two repeated words: Cho Cho, San San, and Ni Ni. Myint means "high" (to clarify: as in "elevated"), Cho means "sweet," San means "new" or "novel," and Ni means "red." Unlike my parents, my great-grandparents did not have too much time on their hands to construct a story about their daughters being elevated, novel, sweet, and red. But you can tell that they did want their daughters' names to reflect good things. My mom's name, Thet, means "life," and during one random fight over how my mom's name came to be Thet Thet, A May sighed and said, "What are you talking about? Of course I remember why I named you Thet Thet. It's because I loved my child more than life itself, so I was calling you my life." Mom didn't have a retort.

In spite of the amount of attention that your parents put into picking out your name, when I was growing up, there was a prevalent trend among my friends to pick out a Western nickname for themselves. My friend Khin can still recall when, on her first day of school, she was handed a book of alphabetized Western names to choose from, so as to help (*cough*, cater to) the American teachers at our school. Up until she graduated from high school, she went by Anna; I called her this for eleven years. She only ditched Anna once she went to the United States for college and wanted to ground herself more firmly in her cultural heritage, and it looks so weird to even write it out now. I've technically known her as Anna for longer than I've known her as Khin, but I can't even physically say the name Anna when I'm talking to or about her anymore. It's a bizarre childhood anecdote that we ponder over from time to time: Who was Anna?

There's a great sketch in *Key & Peele* where a class of high schoolers who come from predominantly white, middle-class backgrounds are one day taught by Mr. Garvey, a new substitute teacher who has spent his career teaching inner-city children. He begins class by going through roll call. "Jay-KWAY-lin?" he asks, as a young girl called Jacqueline attempts to correct him; Mr. Garvey refuses to believe that that's how the name is pronounced. Next, he calls on "Buh-LAH-kay," who responds, "My name's Blake"; Mr. Garvey throws down his clipboard and asks, "Are you out of your goddamn mind?" Next, he reads, "Dee-nice," and the camera pans to a blond girl who is sheepishly looking around with her head down, unsure of if and how to respond. Finally, she says, "Do you mean Denise?" Mr. Garvey breaks his clipboard in half and demands, "You say your name right, right now," and the girl again responds, "Denise."

"Say it right."

"Denise?"

"Correctly?"

"Denise."

"Right."

"Denise."

"Right."

Finally, Denise shakes her head, bites her tongue, and says, "Dee-nice."

Mr. Garvey is satisfied.

Once when I was younger, I asked my mom if I could choose a new name. When she asked me why, I explained that none of my teachers ever knew how to pronounce it. I was privileged enough to attend an international school where one of the biggest selling points was that all the classes were taught by Westerners (usually from the United States, a few from Australia and the United Kingdom, and a handful from other predominantly white countries). My first-grade homeroom teacher was a woman named Ms. Win, and she was the only

Myanmar head teacher I had. Each class also had an assistant teacher, and they were all Myanmar, but apart from Ms. Win, all the other head teachers were white. Of course, Ms. Win and the assistant teachers never had a problem pronouncing "Pyae Pyae," but I instead focused on the fact that my white teachers just couldn't seem to make that one-syllable sound; they didn't know how to pronounce a lot of our names, but mine was always especially difficult. I hated the first day of the school year because during roll call I'd have to brace myself for that awkward silence, followed by "Um . . . Pie Pie?" I'd raise my hand and correct them with a weak smile, although most of them still wouldn't be able to pronounce it correctly.

"How do you say it?"

"Pyae Pyae."

"Again."

"Puh-yay, puh-yay."

"Pee pee?"

Close, but not exactly. Ultimately, I'd nod and bite my tongue, and although we both knew that they hadn't gotten it right, they'd just leave it at that. As an adult, I once shared this story with a group of friends, specifically recalling how messed up it was that I'd felt from a young age that I should *cater to* my white teachers; one person in the group, a white man, spoke up and said it felt melodramatic to use that specific phrase, especially in regard to something as innocent as elementary school roll call. I felt anger shoot through me as I remembered how, regardless of how many times I repeated this ritual, I'd always feel guilty that it was because of me that roll call was taking so long. These teachers wouldn't have stumbled on Blake or Jacqueline or Denise. My stupid name was holding everyone up. Even at the age of six, I felt so sure that it was *my name* that had to change. And when Khin went by Anna, and others went by Louis and Paul and John, none of our white teachers ever questioned it; I don't know if this was because they wanted to respect our choices or because, secretly, they were relieved and maybe even a bit thankful (I am tempted to give them the benefit of the doubt and lean toward the former explanation).

I remember once going through Tripadvisor feedback for a hotel in town, and one of the five-star reviews thanked the staff in the lounge for using Western names and making life easier for them during their stay. I find myself thinking about that review a lot more than I should, and about the audacity of being a visitor in another country and encouraging an establishment to make people who were very clearly not a Susan or a Joe ditch their real names while working. Then again, I also think a lot about how much easier and less stressful a lot of social interactions would be if I just went by Moe. Moe Thet War is easy to say when you break it down, but still too much for non-Myanmar people to handle, and Pyae Pyae just straight-up terrifies them; but Moe is a good middle ground, and I could probably break the ice with some joke from *The Simpsons*. And yet I really don't like it when someone calls me Moe. I'm not offended, but it feels strange and jarring, like a stranger calling me by a childhood nickname. I am Moe Thet War and I am Pyae Pyae, but I am not Moe.

You see, just as Toothpick's mom was wrapping her head around the fact that (1) I was not baptized and (2) I did not have a christened Christian name, she then had to also process the fact that I didn't have a middle or last name either. Myanmar families typically don't have shared last names, and we never have middle names. So technically, Pyae Pyae and Moe Thet War are each just one big name. If I were to go by Moe Thet War, my family and friends would call me by my whole name, not just Moe. When white people point out that that's weird or sounds like a mouthful, I like to point out that Elizabeth itself has more syllables than Moe Thet War, and no one feels like it's a chore to say Elizabeth Taylor.

When we had to sign up for APs and SATs in high school, I had to decide what name I wanted on my file. Our high school counselor, a tall, lanky white American man in his mid-forties we called Mr. Mike, spent every day stressing to each of us over and over again how crucial it was that we put down the same things for our first, middle, and last names on every single form. It sounded easy enough, but some of us didn't get why we had to divide up our names; it was like asking someone named Edward to divide up his name into Ed, Wa, and Rd.

The first time I took a mock PSAT, my hand hovered over that first all-important blank box on that seemingly forever-binding form. I went to write "Moe" as my first name and "Thet" as my middle name—the logical choice—but then I paused. That would mean that my name would appear as "Moe T. War." That looked wrong. The *T* was important. The *T* gave birth to me. When I was switching schools and the principal wanted me to repeat a grade because I was too young, the *T* vouched for me and dared him to test me on any subject because *I know my daughter and I know what she's capable of.* The *T* made the best spaghetti Bolognese.

I put down "Moe Thet," two words, as my first name. That looked better. I knew that most traditional (Western) names didn't have two names in the first box, but to me, this was what looked right.

About a decade or so later, when I was trying to figure out what name I wanted to publish my first book (this book) under, I tossed and turned in bed for weeks—yet another identity crisis (I thought I'd be done with those by my mid-twenties) not dissimilar to the one I experienced over that PSAT form. I'd always assumed that if and when I became a published author, I'd publish under Moe Thet War because that just made the paperwork less complicated. Now, however, it was less of a clear choice. For one, I didn't want to have to keep explaining to all the new people I'd work with why I went by Pyae Pyae instead of what was printed on my book cover, and second—and more pressingly—I realized it would be almost dishonest to fulfill a lifelong dream while neglecting such a central part of my identity. I'd imagine my friends going into a bookstore and saying, "That's Pyae's book," and it felt bizarre to imagine them holding up "Pyae's book" without "Pyae" printed anywhere on the cover. I wish I could go back and tell my elementary school self who wanted to replace Pyae Pyae with something like Lizzie (after McGuire, obviously) that in a couple of decades, she would make an entirely voluntary choice to have "Pyae" printed on the front of her debut book.

When I was twelve, my mom came home one evening after a round of parent-teacher conferences with a puzzled look on her face. I was worried that it was something to do with my report card, which I had yet to see, but her concern was instead directed at my sister.

"Shan?" she asked my then-eight-year-old sister. "Are you going by 'Rose' at school?"

My sister nodded but offered no further explanation, unsure why this was a topic of conversation.

"I only found out when your teacher showed me your work today and it all had the name 'Rose' on it. Why did you choose 'Rose'?"

"Because you always say that when I was born, I was so pink and beautiful like a hnin si flower. And hnin si in English is 'rose.'"

It was a logical response, one that my mom couldn't really argue against, but after hearing my sister's reply, I also shared Mom's confusion. Shan was a perfectly good name. It wasn't even difficult for her American teachers to pronounce. What was wrong with it? To this day, I don't think even she knows the answer.

For the next seven years, my baby sister went by Shan at home and Rose at school. When we talked about her with family, we called her Shan, and with her friends, Rose. It almost morphed into a fun Hannah Montana-esque double life for her.

The thing was, though, the Pyae–Phyo–Shan concept didn't work with Pyae–Phyo–Rose. And it was especially crucial to my mother that, unlike her and her own brothers, my siblings and I never lose one another. On their passports today, my mother and her older brother, whom we call Ba Ba, actually share their father's last name, Naing—although that wasn't always the case. A May says that they were forced to change Ba Ba and Mom's last names to Naing because when they moved to New York for my grandfather's job, they were legally required to have an official surname. My mom and uncle(s) are more legally bound on paper than my siblings and I will ever be—they are the Naings, a single entity—and yet my mother sees her older brother twice a year and she rarely speaks about her younger one.

Oftentimes, though, to white people, it doesn't matter if your whole family has the same Western-style last name if that last name—or any part of your name, for that matter—is still a very obvious non-white, non-European one. A two-year study on the usage of "whitened résumés" by people of color showed that the percentage of Asian job applicants who heard back from prospective employers dropped from 21 percent to 11.5 percent if they sent résumés with racial references, such as, say, a blatantly non-Western name. Multiple other studies have been conducted on this topic over the years, and each time, the overarching results are the same.

The thing with names is that they don't seem like such a big deal until you really think about them and what they represent, or until everyone else makes it a big deal. Shakespeare argued that "a rose by any other name would smell as sweet," which is pretty inaccurate, because if I had a white name, then my childhood and early teenage years would've involved a lot less self-hatred. To this day, I can still recall how much I despised the fact that I could never teach my teachers to twist their tongues to correctly pronounce this one syllable once, never mind twice. Of course, any other name seems equally easy and sweet when you've got a name like William, or better yet, Bill. I've been in situations where everyone could keep track of who was Meghan and who was Megan, and yet my name appeared too convoluted for them to even attempt to say aloud.

At one point in my late teens, I was arrogant enough to think that I was so much wiser, and I would berate my thirteen-year-old self for wanting to adopt a Western name for (apparently) no good reason. "What a self-loathing kid I was," I'd say to people when I told them the story. Then I began dipping my toe in the *real* world and suddenly there was scientific research claiming that maybe going by Lizzie wouldn't be the worst idea, especially if I wanted to have the career I was pursuing. I wanted to work as an English-language writer in some capacity, and the reality was that my name was enough to prompt potential employers to question my language skills or make professors hesitant about letting me into their higher-level literature classes. The name of the rose did—does—matter.

In Myanmar, names are composed of two or more actual words from the language. Moe means "rain," Thet means "life," and War means "yellow." So my name, literally translated, is "Rain Life Yellow." But we transliterate our names into English; the upside to this is that I'm not referred to as Rain Life Yellow, but the downside is that sometimes people learn my supposed "last name" and start singing the Edwin Starr song as though it's the most original joke in the world (to which I ask, "What *is* it good for?"). Everyone from new professors to particularly chatty restaurant servers who aren't Myanmar or aren't familiar with the culture always note that I have a cool last name in War, which then leads to them asking me if there's a story behind my name. I know it comes from a place of curiosity, but years of this conversation made me internalize the notion that my name is "weird" because, well, you don't ask for the story behind something that isn't strange. No one says, "The reservation's under Andrew," and then spends the first two minutes of the meal having to explain to their waitress, "Well, it's derived from the Greek *Andreas*, which can be further traced back to the Ancient Greek word for *man* ..." Names are packed with cultural and emotional significance and are almost always more than *just* a name, but sometimes I wish that people would see or read or hear my name and ask only how to pronounce it correctly, foregoing the rest of the director's commentary and letting it be just that: a name.

When I introduce myself to someone new who isn't Myanmar, they often tell me that I have a beautiful name, even though my name could literally mean "fart fart" and they wouldn't have a clue. In the 1963 novel *Hopscotch* (or *Rayuela* in the original Spanish) by Argentine writer Julio Cortázar, the protagonist pulls out a list of Myanmar names that, to him, seemingly have no meaning, but that still appear alluring and exotic, and with which he "could not resist the temptation to take out a pencil and compose the following nonsense poem:

U Nu,
U Tin,
Mya Bu,
Thado Thiri Thudama U E Maung,
Sithu U Cho,
Wunna Kyaw Htin U Khin Zaw,
Wunna Kyaw Htin U Thein Han,
Wunna Kyaw Htin U Myo Min,
Thiri Pyanchi U Thant,
Thado Maha Thray Sithu U Chan Htoon."

I read these names and I know both how to pronounce each one and what each one means, and I have to remind myself that a lot of people don't. To a lot of people, my name could very easily just be a fun, thoughtless addition to a nonsense poem. They think my name sounds beautiful when I say it, or when I write it down on a piece of paper, but they get squeamish when they're forced to say it themselves. I try to be gentle and guide them: "It's like 'yay' with a *P* in front." I give a warm smile, like I'm encouraging a child to take their first step. *You can do it!* I want to cheer. *It's so easy, it's one syllable! I have so much faith in you!*

I remember one afternoon during my second year of college when I was seventeen and sitting in my dorm room and fiddling around on the internet because I was putting off doing the reading for my epistemology class, which I only signed up for because I loved the professor. A few clicks led me to an interview with the actress Uzo Aduba in which she was asked if she'd ever considered changing her name. Her answer was a resolute "No," and then she went on to explain why. I found out that like "Pyae Pyae" in Myanmar, "Uzoamaka" also means something in Nigerian culture ("The road is good"), and like my family did, her mother also gave her a name that she hoped would set the foundation for a bright future. And then—and I remember pausing for several seconds as I read this last bit, as every feeling I'd ever had toward my name, from pride to hatred to embarrassment to confusion, collided into one another and crystallized into something manageable for the first time—she said that her mother told her when she was a kid, "If they can learn to say Tchaikovsky and Michelangelo and Dostoyevsky, they can learn to say Uzoamaka." I know it's peculiar to admit that I think about Uzo Aduba's mother a lot, but in another universe where I get to meet her, I imagine myself thanking her for saying those words to her daughter to repeat in an interview decades later and helping me undo a knot of guilt and shame that a decade and a half of internalized racism had tightly wound together.

A few years ago, I found a 1958 article in *The Atlantic* simply titled "Burmese Names," and subtitled "A guide." While most of the piece was a primer on Myanmar names that reiterated everything I knew, I was amused at the line: "'What's in a name?' the saying goes, and perhaps Burmese feel this more than other peoples, for, if one of us in [*sic*] dogged by bad luck or ill health he won't hesitate to choose a new one, simply putting an announcement in the paper that he has done so." I had never heard this tidbit before, but if you know Myanmar people, it honestly does sound like something we would do.

Moe Thet War, also known as Pyae Pyae, changed her legal name to Lizzie Marie War at the Yangon Western District Court at 3:00 p.m., Wednesday, November 12, 2008. The document signing was officiated by a clerk from the Department of Name Alterations for People Who Are Running from the Law, and Cultural Traitors.

Lizzie, after attending a weeklong meditation retreat to prepare for a lifetime of passive-aggressive remarks from her parents, will settle in Yangon as she finishes up her studies.

Up until the late twentieth century, Myanmar was known as Burma, and other variations of Burma that have appeared in previous atlases and literary works include "Burmah," "Birmah," and "Bermah." In July 1989, forty-one years after the country gained independence, the name was officially changed to the Union of Myanmar, in an attempt to more formally detach the country from its colonial past; the same changes were made with a number of towns and cities throughout the country, most notably of the then-capital Rangoon to Yangon, the latter a combination of the words "yan" ("enemies") and "kone" ("to be out of something"). Several streets in Yangon were also officially (re)named as distinctly Myanmar streets: Godwin Road, which commemorated Sir Henry Thomas Godwin, the commander in chief of the British and Indian Forces in the Second Anglo-Burmese War, became Lanmadaw Road, "lanmadaw" literally translating to "the royal road," for it was this road that King Tharrawaddy took when he marched into Yangon in 1841; Dalhousie Road was renamed Maha Bandoola Road, the former honoring Lord Dalhousie, who served as governor-general of India from 1848 to 1856, and the latter, a Myanmar general who helped lead the fight against the British in the First Anglo-Burmese War; Montgomery Road, named after a sergeant in the British Army, transformed into Bogyoke Aung San Road, after Aung San Suu Kyi's father, who was instrumental in the country's fight for independence and was infamously assassinated during a cabinet meeting.

But in addition to shedding traces of our colonial history, changes such as Rangoon to Yangon stemmed from the simple fact that certain letters and sounds, such as the *r* sound, do not exist in the Myanmar language; Rangoon and Burma solely catered to a British, English-speaking community. When I'm asked about the difference between Burma and Myanmar, the simple answer is that one name was given to us by the British, and the other was picked out by a new Myanmar government; the complex answer is that one name was what we were known as under British rule, and the other by a new military government who wanted to proclaim their control on this newly liberated country—and what better way to assert your power than by literally changing the nation's entire name? On a day-to-day basis, though, we ourselves used to and continue to use Bama colloquially as both a proper noun and an adjective (for instance, the Bama language), and unless you work in politics, it's not necessarily viewed as an indication of colonial glorification. Bama, Burma. Yangon, Rangoon. Pyae Pyae, Pee Pee. What's in a name, indeed?

I've been with Toothpick for over half a decade now, and one of the few secrets that I have from him is that he still cannot, and probably will never, pronounce "Pyae" correctly. I am constantly aware of it, but will never voice it; I know it's not intentional, and that if he could take lessons in Saying My Name 101, he'd sign up in an instant. If he were to bring it up, I'd reassure him that he shouldn't feel bad because none of my non-Myanmar friends pronounce my name accurately either.

"It's a soft *P*," I would explain to him.

What's a soft *P*?

"Well, the way you're saying it, it's a hard *P*."

How?

"It's soft, as in *spit* or *top*. The *p* is there, but you don't really say it. If you pronounced the *p* in *spit*, you'd physically spit out the word."

I try not to think about the fact that a person, *the* person, my person, who knows me inside out and outside in, will never know how to say my name correctly. I can't recall if I've ever heard him murmur my name in his sleep. I've never had that moment with a partner, to have my name be so normal and part of his everyday vocabulary that his brain and mouth know how to make that sound without even meaning to.

I know he loves my name—I am his favorite person, and my name is his favorite one to see pop up when his phone rings—but I also know that if we weren't dating, he'd be one of his friends who regularly asks, "Sorry to do this, but how do you say your girlfriend's name again?" My name will never be on the tip of his tongue.

I'm sorry my name is so difficult to say. I'm sorry, I'm sorry, I'm sorry.

I wrote the very first draft of this essay in 2012, during my sophomore year of college. Out of all the things I've written from when I was seventeen to the present day, this is the one piece that for some reason I always circle back to. Every few months for the last eightish years, I've opened the Word document on my computer and tinkered with it here and there. It was first written as an assignment for the first creative writing workshop I'd ever taken, one in which I was the only non-white person. At the time, I was living in a small, very white American town. Saying my name aloud to my new friends and professors and colleagues was an almost-embarrassing ordeal the first few weeks of my freshman year, and I felt like I was in elementary school all over again, mad at myself for holding up roll call. By the time I wrote this essay, though, I was nearing the end of my sophomore year and I'd come to love my name—there were so many Sarahs and Saras and even one Sahra on campus, but literally no other Pyae Pyae—and it felt cathartic to finally be processing all the emotions that I'd ever felt toward my name. Now, at twenty-five, I don't yell my name from the rooftops, but I do politely but firmly insist that you call me by my name. I'm not embarrassed to repeat it a few times when I'm introducing myself to a new group of people; I say it again and again, and maybe again, determined that they say it too until they get it right. Sometimes I take it out on Toothpick by putting him on the spot when he mumbles his way through someone else's non-Western name or gives up and says, "Ugh, I can't remember their name right now." I yell, "No! You *do* remember it, you just don't want to try to pronounce it because it's not white!" When we saw *Avengers: Endgame*, I refused to let him get away with pretending he didn't know how to say Danai Gurira when he had no problem pronouncing Benedict fucking Cumberbatch; I am thankful and happy that Danai Gurira has not adopted an easier name for her career, that neither did Uzo Aduba, nor did I.

"What do you think of my name?" I asked him recently, as I was revisiting this essay in its most recent incarnation. I was trying to formulate my own collective thoughts on the topic at this moment in my life, and had realized that it'd been a while since I'd sat down and thought of my name for an extended period of time.

"What? Pyae?" he responded, confused.

"Yeah. What do you think of it?"

Without missing a beat, he said, "It's your name, therefore I love it."

LAUNDRY LOAD

am embarrassed to admit that I have, on more than one occasion, paid what is objectively an obscene amount of money for a single piece of underwear; often I call up one of my best friends, either Poe or Khin, a few minutes later and lament, "It's not fair! Why do the tiniest pieces of fabric always cost the most?!" This is a long-standing grudge of mine against the general women's undergarment industry—namely, I don't understand why women's underwear costs so much when, again, the priciest items are intentionally designed so as to barely cover your nipples or crotch or butt crack. Reading the *Gossip Girl* books as a teenager, I noticed that Blair Waldorf wore underwear and lingerie only from La Perla and I thought to myself that *I* wanted to be the kind of girl who wore only La Perla—that is, until I bounced into a La Perla store on one afternoon and immediately bounced back out after seeing the triple-digit number on the price tag of a single pair of briefs. But I like to treat myself to pretty underwear that's made of lace and satin and occasionally silk, and when I throw my more expensive underwear in the washer, I make sure to put them in a separate garment mesh wash bag, and afterward, I make sure to air-dry them instead of tossing them in the dryer. I was taught that the men of a household should never have to do the laundry, which is, of course, fucked up, but you know what? I *do* do most, if not all, of the laundry in my relationship, not because I don't want a poor man to have to exert himself by throwing items into a machine and pressing a few buttons, but because I like clean clothes (it is mind-boggling how high guys will let stuff pile up!), and, more important, because I don't trust an adult man to properly wash and dry my clothing, including, and especially, my fifty-dollar panties.

And every time I *do* combine my washing with that of a man—usually a partner, maybe a friend if they're staying over—I feel like a little smug, rebellious piece of shit. I've never cared about separating whites and colors when I do laundry, nor have I ever been taught to care; instead, what I *have* been taught, even before I learned which drawer the detergent goes in, is that men's and women's clothes must always, always, until-the-day-I-die-always be separated, even when they're put in a laundry hamper, and certainly when they're being washed. I like to mess around with Mom and sometimes do things *just* to spite her, having become very good at rolling my eyes while drowning out any subsequent scolding, but my voice gets caught in my throat every time I even *think* of telling her that I have, and do, wash my clothes, including my underwear, in the same laundry load as a man's; that yes, I have done this on many occasions, and yes, if I were to get married one day, I would do this with my husband's laundry, too. I don't see how or why this would even ever come up in casual conversation—it's not like we sit around talking about all the laundry we did this week—but nonetheless, it feels like my version of "The Tell-Tale Heart" that I am actually a tiny bit scared she'll find out about one day.

The Myanmar concept of hpone refers to this innate, mystical power that men supposedly possess, and that is believed to be sapped if, among other examples, men's clothes come in contact with women's. Hpone is applicable not just in laundry but across all aspects of our culture, including, for instance, religion. It's believed that only a (cisgender) man can become the next Buddha because only men have hpone; as a result, only men can touch the Buddha statues at the pagodas, and there are certain areas at most pagodas that women are forbidden from entering. While a woman could never possess as much hpone as a man, she can rob the latter of his, or at least reduce his hpone by, for instance, making a man sleep on the floor while she sleeps on a bed or sofa or inhabits any space that is physically (and thus metaphorically) higher than his. I imagine this is what it must be like when you live with, say, the pope, except imagine how exhausting it is to have to treat *every single man* that you know with the same reverence as you do the pope.

Hpone is also the reason why a lot of Myanmar households never wash men's and women's clothing together, nor hang them up to dry on the same rack. In the hallway outside my parents' bedroom are four tall plastic baskets, two positioned on each side of the door. I was taught early on that one pair of baskets was for my mom's clothes, and the other for my dad's; the same was true for my brother's clothing in respect to mine and my sister's. Our clothes could never be washed in the same wash because that would negatively impact my father's or my brother's hpone. Because women's clothing, particularly underwear and garments worn on the lower part of the body (such as skirts, trousers, or hta meins), are unclean, they especially could rob a man of his hpone if they came in contact with said man's clothes; if my mother's hta mein were washed in the same wash as my dad's pa soe, my dad's hpone would be hurt as a result. If we played in the backyard where the laundry was hung up to dry, A May would keep a close eye on my brother to make sure he didn't run under any of the poles that had the women's clothing on them, lest our underwear graze the top of his head.

From an objective standpoint, the concept of hpone and its many rules sound sexist and baseless (and they are), but the fear of diminishing a man's hpone is one that almost all Myanmar people hold. In 2015, a woman was arrested after she shared a cartoon of then–newly appointed state counselor Aung San Suu Kyi and military commander in chief Min Aung Hlaing on Facebook and commented that if the commander in chief *loved* the state counselor so much, he should wear her hta mein as a bandana around his head. Min Aung Hlaing was outraged that a woman dared even make a joke that would imply a lessening of his hpone and took her to court, and the defendant was found guilty under an antidefamation law that landed her a six-month prison sentence.

As the oldest child, I was always told that I needed to get along with my brother and sister because I would be left in charge of them if something were to happen to my parents. And yet, even though I was at the top of the hierarchy, I was also taught from a young age that my little brother was inherently and spiritually *better*. Whenever I questioned these rules, my mom would shut me down and reply, "Well, whether you like it or not, we are Myanmar." She was right. It was—is—ingrained into our culture that men are innately superior to women, and while I suspect many women know that it's wrong, it's difficult to undo a lifetime of social conditioning. In 2019, a male Myanmar artist held an exhibition in which he challenged this belief that men's and women's laundry couldn't be washed together. But while it seemed that several older women knew it was sexist and outdated, they still couldn't teach themselves to unlearn a decades-old practice. One viewer admitted, "Even now, I continue to follow the custom; however, I will teach my own children that it is wrong."

In our family specifically, it was even more crucial to separate our laundry because, as in most military families, my mom followed the widely held belief that it would be bad luck for a soldier if he, or his clothes, were somehow soiled by coming in contact with women's clothing. My dad joined the army long before I was born, so growing up, he was often posted to different parts of the country. He did, however, come home every few months, and in that time, my mother wasn't going to risk leaving her children fatherless by not separating their clothing just because she was too lazy, or because she wanted to make a statement in the name of feminism.

When my dad was away, Mom and A May kept things running. My mother worked to pay for everything while A May did the housework. It is fitting that I call my grandma A May because I did—do—essentially have two mothers. Mom worked five days a week, attended all the parent-teacher conferences, and she was always on top of Tooth Fairy and Santa duty. A May taught us how to read and write as well as basic math, did all the grocery shopping, and cooked all our meals. Every morning, Mom would make the rounds through our three bedrooms and wake up each one of us, getting our backpacks ready while we crawled out of bed, and A May would fry rice and bacon in the kitchen. By the time we were showered and dressed and came downstairs, Mom would plate our breakfast while A May packed our lunches. If something needed to be fixed around the house, they busted out the toolbox and mended it themselves. I had a lot more admiration and respect for A May and my mother than I did my father or my grandfather, and so it confounded me that they assumed that they were nonetheless *spiritually* inferior to these men, neither of whom were around to help them feed, teach, and raise three young children.

I have never resented my father for his career choices and the consequent fact that he wasn't around for the majority of our childhood; regardless of how far away he was or how long he was gone, I knew that he thought about us all the time. I have no doubt that my father loves me more than his masculine ego would ever admit, and that he thinks I'm capable of doing anything I put my mind to. But during those brief visits before he left his job and permanently moved back in with us, and before I was even aware of the concept of feminism, I would, however, notice and resent how the hierarchy of the house instantly transformed whenever he came home, and, specifically, that his authority would trump that of A May and Mom as he reclaimed his title as the man of the house.

I sometimes still feel that resentment bubble back up when I go over to my parents' house, especially if it's for a family meal. My spot at their circular dining table places me in front of the cutlery drawers, and when we eat, Dad likes to sit right beside me. If he needs a spoon or a fork, though, he'll ask me to get it for him; and even though it would merely require me to stretch out my hand and get it out of the drawer behind me, I refuse every time.

"Pyae, get it for him," Mom scolds me from across the room.

And every time, I say, "No. He has hands too. It's the same distance from both of our seats."

And then she lets out an exasperated sigh, walks over to us, and gets his cutlery out for him.

This exchange has happened more often than it should—my father asking me to get him a spoon, me always saying no, my mother scolding me and getting the spoon herself. When I refuse to give my father his cutlery, Mom laughs and half-scolds me: "Kaung kaung nay." Be good.

"I worry about you so much," she used to tell me when I was a teenager. She would say it randomly, when it was just the two of us, sitting in the car or watching TV.

"What are you worried about?" I'd ask.

"You don't know anything. I worry that someone will take advantage of you or hurt you one day." We both knew that by *anything*, she meant anything about men, and that by *someone*, she also meant men. I didn't know men, didn't know my place in relation to them, and my ignorance would possibly one day result in a man teaching me my place. She had sent me to an international school from a young age because she wanted me to get the best education possible, but she also worried over the years about what I was being taught at this school, and what ideas and rules my American teachers were passing on to me.

Her fears only increased when I moved to the United States for college. My parents wanted me to go to the other side of the world because they felt an American degree was my key to a better future, but A May prayed up to the day of my departure. She was scared I would be kidnapped and then held for ransom, or sold off into slavery, or murdered, or some combination of the three. She was also scared that I would change, and when I came home in the summer and winter during our school breaks, she observed my every move, making note of all the big and small ways in which the West had altered her teenage granddaughter, beyond the 300 percent increase in my overall pasta consumption, that is.

I don't think it's hyperbolic to say that in the context of my cultural upbringing, arguably the worst Western concept I was exposed to, and consequently *bought into*, was that of feminism. In my freshman year, our college organized a van for anyone who wanted to go to New York City to attend the city's first-ever SlutWalk, which, I learned, was a march that protested rape culture and called out harmful social norms such as victim blaming and slut shaming, especially in regard to sexual assault victims. Bianca, one of the first friends I made at college, was a young self-proclaimed feminist and asked if I wanted to attend with her; I said no for fear that something would go awry and I would be arrested and risk losing my visa; Bianca went, complete with handmade signs and a skimpy outfit that consisted of just her bra and a pair of Daisy Duke shorts. I was in awe.

That year, I also attended my first-ever production of Eve Ensler's *The Vagina Monologues*. One of the lines in the introduction is "We were worried about vaginas, what we call them and don't call them." In Myanmar culture, you don't refer to your vagina unless you absolutely have to, such as for medical reasons, and I can tell you from experience that even then, in a room with just the two of you, the doctor will lower her voice to a hushed tone. During a consultation to book a medical checkup, a female doctor strongly insisted to my friend, a young, single woman, that it was unnecessary for her to get a Pap smear due to her marital status, hinting that such a procedure would be uncomfortable for an unmarried woman. In 2015, *The Myanmar Times* ran a seemingly innocuous article in which the writer—a white woman—pointed out that the name of a traditional Myanmar snack, ar pon, is also slang for *vagina*, and that in English, the snack could technically be called vagina snack; a few days later, after several flabbergasted readers had voiced their outrage over the fact that a colloquialism for vagina had been so crassly printed in black and white, the paper printed an apology that read: "*Myanmar Times* chief executive Tony Child apologizes for the choice of snack on page six of The Supplement on October 16 which is described by an indecent word in the Myanmar language." Women's hta meins and underwear are deemed inferior and dirty specifically because they come in contact with a vagina. Up until my late teens—when I finally went on the internet and did my own research—I wouldn't have known if something was wrong with my vagina because I didn't have a baseline as to what a normal, healthy vagina was supposed to look or feel or smell like. I didn't even know what the different parts of a vagina were until then; Bianca talked to me about the *clit* once and I said, "What?" and she explained it to me. "What if a guy doesn't know what that is?" I asked, and she smirked and said, "Don't worry, he'll know." I once told my mom that your vagina and your urinary tract are two different things, and she said that that was ridiculous; I realized then that, at eighteen,

I knew more about vaginas than my own mother. She also didn't let me present further evidence for my argument because she didn't want to hear any more talk of vaginas. Fuck, it even feels wrong to write about clitorises and urethras and just vaginas on the whole—what if my mother actually *reads* this?

I do not know who were the first men who came up with this opinion that vaginas are dirty and bad, but it had to be men, and they preached it enough that it became ingrained in our culture. Each time I came home from college, I recognized with a shock the small and large ways in which misogyny permeated Myanmar culture, one of the most glaring examples being the absurdity of the strange, sexist laundry rule. To voice my thoughts, however, also made me feel as though I was going against my culture, as though I was positing Western ideas as better and more progressive. I could read as much Western literature as I wanted, but at the end of the day, I was Myanmar. My grandfather used to be a diplomat, and he, A May, Ba Ba, and Mom would live in different countries depending on where he was assigned. Regardless of where my grandfather's job took them, A May never forgot that they were Myanmar; in all the photos of them from their time abroad, A May is wearing a hta mein, and when her spouse and children came home, she cooked them Myanmar food, and they all spoke Myanmar. And even in New York City, where I'm sure her

American friends would've mocked her for adhering to such a misogynistic rule, A May would've still separated her and my mom's clothes from those of my uncle and grandpa. *It's just what we do. We are Myanmar.*

Toothpick first visited Myanmar after we'd been together for over three years. His trip also overlapped with the thirty-third WrestleMania, which is something we like to watch together every year. Due to the time difference between Yangon and Florida, where it was being held that year, the show started stupidly early in Yangon time, and he sat down on one end of my couch while I lay down, my head at the other end of the couch and my feet in his lap. I dozed in and out between matches, and would occasionally nudge his cheek with my foot to ask him to get me a glass of water or some snacks—which he did, no questions asked. I should've been used to it by that point, but even there in the privacy and security of my own home, whispers of my impacting his hpone— women aren't supposed to touch a man's head with their foot—invaded my brain, even as I was half asleep. And yet it was a strange feeling—not just that of equality, but also of being with a man who didn't feel less of a man because his female partner nudged him with her foot and asked him to get her some food. I remembered my mom's fears for me and I wished she could've been there in that moment so I could show her: *You don't have to worry. He would never hurt me.*

Sometimes—and I'm utterly ashamed of myself whenever I even think this—I am grateful that I've never dated a Myanmar man. Obviously, I acknowledge that I have also just been lucky and fallen in love with some very good men who also happen to not be Myanmar, but I wonder if even the best Myanmar man would be as good as Toothpick, or if they would always expect me to get them a spoon and have two separate hampers. I love being Myanmar, but it pains me that a culture and group of people that I love so much doesn't love me as much as it does my brother or my father. It would be unfair and inaccurate to say that Western cultures have nailed gender equality, and there are Myanmar men who, like me, have tried their hardest to unlearn everything they were taught about hpone, but I am still grappling with how to love a culture that, at least in this aspect, still promotes a belief that is hurtful, discriminatory, and wrong. I don't want to make the blanket statement that Myanmar culture hates women, but it doesn't love us, not unconditionally, and sometimes it seems like it will respect other men before it respects its own women. During his trip, along with my parents and some family friends, Toothpick and I took the three-hour drive from Yangon to Kyaiktiyo Pagoda, which sits on a giant gold-covered boulder perched on the edge of a cliff. There is a small bridge that separates the boulder from the rest of the mountain, and only men are allowed to cross it. When we went, Dad and his friends took Toothpick up to the boulder so he could participate in the tradition of sticking gold leaves onto it.

"You're not coming?" Toothpick turned and asked me, assuming I wasn't joining him because I wasn't interested.

"I'm not allowed," I replied. He was confused. I repeated, clarifying, "Women aren't allowed."

"It felt wrong," Toothpick still says, years later. "I'm not even religious. I didn't get why I was allowed to touch it and women who were Buddhists couldn't."

In a 1958 article in *The Atlantic* titled "The Women of Burma," writer Daw Mya Sein observed that while there are certain cultural situations in which it is obvious that men are more respected than women, she ultimately concluded:

> Burmese women occupy a privileged and independent position . . . which is not limited either by marriage or by motherhood, and which allows us, eventually, to fit ourselves into the life, the work, and all the rewards that our country has to offer equally with our men.

I've heard this sentiment echoed by female friends who are proud of their Myanmar heritage: "Myanmar women don't take their husbands' last names, we run businesses right beside our husbands, and if you look at us on the whole, it does all seem like a challenge to the stereotype of the quiet, demure, submissive Asian woman." I get it—it's tough to acknowledge the ugly sides of someone or something that you love, especially when there simultaneously exist so many examples that indicate otherwise. Mothers and grandmothers are revered for giving you life, and you might even call an older woman who isn't your biological (grand)mother May May or A May as a sign of respect. It was a woman who carried on the great Bogyoke Aung San's fight for democracy. A man will catcall and grope you in the street, but then go home and proudly defend his sister's honor and demonstrate that he has her back if another man does the same to her. And when people from white, Western cultures denounce ours as a backward environment where primitive misogynistic myths still run rampant (because obviously there is no sexism in, say, American society), Myanmar women, including myself, are tempted to point at all the ways in which we do admire and applaud our women and their contributions to society. It's a wonderful picture to proudly display: "For centuries—even before recorded history, from all we can deduce—Burmese women have accepted as their right a high measure of independence." *So why*, I want to ask, *are the men allowed to touch pagodas, but we aren't? Why can't I walk over my brother's legs if they're stretched out on the floor? Why can't we throw our underwear in the same wash if I'm being nice enough to do everyone's fucking laundry in the first place?*

There's a common belief that the human body will have replaced every cell in seven years, meaning that after that period of time, you will quite literally be a different person. The truth, though, is that you will have shed all the cells in your old stomach lining in two to nine days, and your outer layer of skin in two to four weeks; your red blood cells take about four months to replace themselves; and it turns out that it actually takes ten years for you to have a completely new skeleton. However, that doesn't mean that you are entirely new. In reality, half of your heart, the majority of your brain, and the core of your eye lens all remain the same from birth to death. But maybe while the lens through which you see everything will never change, the other half of your heart and the parts of your brain that do renew themselves can reprogram your view of the world.

A friend of mine, Ye, who is about a decade older than me but also attended college in the United States, once recalled to me about his own experience watching *The Vagina Monologues* for the first time. As someone who had been born and raised in Myanmar, like me, he too was fascinated by these women who were talking freely about their vaginas, about how they "don't want [their] pussy to smell like rain. All cleaned up like washing a fish after you cooked it," or how "the clitoris is pure in purpose. It is the only organ in the body designed purely for pleasure." During his third year, at his third viewing, the performance was held in a space where women's underwear was hung up on clotheslines. Even after having spent the last few years on a fairly politically liberal campus, his first instinct was to hesitate to enter the venue because it involved him having to walk under female garments. He did it anyway.

Months into our relationship, Toothpick and I inevitably got to the point where we each had to do laundry at the other's house. The first few times I went to put his clothes in the wash, I caught myself wondering if I should ask him if he'd be okay with me washing our clothes together, with me putting my three-day-old underwear in the same load as his shirts. He had *seemed* unperturbed about putting his clothes in the same hamper as mine, but maybe he would be disgusted by the thought of our underwear being washed together, rubbing against one another in 30°C water for over an hour, and then even longer in the tumble dryer. And even if he himself didn't care at all, two small voices in my head that sounded just like Mom and A May scolded me for doing something that a good Myanmar girl would never do. It felt like a betrayal of my whole culture.

In 2019, eight years after that first viewing of the play at my small liberal arts college in the United States, I attended a local production of *The Vagina Monologues* in Yangon that had been translated and staged by a Myanmar woman my age. As a teenager, I never would've dreamed of seeing posters advertising an exhibition or show or movie or literally *anything* that had the word *vagina* in giant bold letters at the top, and I certainly would've giggled and immediately looked away if someone had invited me to such an event; but I had grown up and was now less embarrassed about womanhood and vaginas, and so had, it appeared, other women my age. I went with Khin and Poe, and while there were, as I expected, a lot of white women in attendance, there were also a lot of Myanmar women. Before the show started, we browsed the two merch tables behind the seating area. I picked up a plain white mug that had, on one side, ပိပိတို့စကားဝိုင်း printed on top and THE VAGINA MONOLOGUES underneath, and on the other, a black-and-white drawing of a vagina, pubic hair and all. My first thought was that I wanted the mug. My second thought was *What will Mom say when she sees it in my cupboard?* After all, dirty vaginas don't belong in clean, sanitary kitchens. I took out a five-thousand-kyat note from my wallet and bought it anyway.

At the peak of my teen feminist angst, I became a strong advocate of the pro-period movement. As a girl who got her first period embarrassingly early in life, I also learned very early that if women's underwear was like a chunk of kryptonite to a man's hpone, period-stained underwear was the literal bleeding core of a kryptonite volcano. As a teenager, Mom would make me put my

43

used pads into opaque black plastic bags and, like a fast-moving ninja, swiftly toss out the bags before my dad next went into the bathroom so as to spare him the horror and embarrassment of coming face-to-face with a bag that contained a woman's used menstruation products.

Sticking to my role of the rebellious teenage feminist, I purchased several pairs of period underwear, which, as the name suggests, is underwear that you wear during your period to soak up your menstrual blood. When washing your period underwear, you first put it under running water and wring out all the blood until the water runs clear, and then you can pop it in with the rest of your laundry. The first time I put my period underwear in the same wash as Toothpick's clothes, I half expected A May to burst through my front door after having sprinted from Yangon to Oxford in a matter of minutes, screaming at the top of her lungs, "Did you learn nothing from me? We are Myanmar! We don't do this!" But of course she didn't, nor did she know, and I just stood there, equally proud of the stigmas I had overcome and ashamed of how I had turned my back on my culture, watching his and my clothing go round and round in my washing machine, my dirty period underwear mixing and getting tangled up with his spiritually superior shirts and defiling his hpone.

To protest the 2021 military coup d'état, women activists launched what became dubbed the Hta Mein

Revolution. In order to deter, or at least slow down, police and military personnel from marching through the streets to break up protests, protestors hung up clotheslines of hta meins and underwear. Because the Myanmar male ego's belief of hpone truly is a curse that was tactfully used against them, in this case, the idea was that the soldiers and police would feel compelled to remove these clotheslines before marching onward (which they did). Imagine that: choosing to stop and hinder your own ability to do your job simply because you are terrified of walking underneath a woman's skirt. In Myanmar, hta mein is spelled ထမိန်, which also means "we rise"—sometimes life and language are just perfect in their natural poetry.

Because it's funny, isn't it—if just a piece of women's underwear has the ability to take away this inherent, almost godlike essence with which men are naturally born, who holds the real power here?

SWIMMING LESSONS

Have you ever met someone who was reincarnated? I don't believe in reincarnation, never really have. I believe that matter is neither created nor destroyed, and find more solace in the thought that when someone you love dies, their body disintegrates and goes back into the earth, and the particles that were once them remain in the world for you to encounter. I don't believe that you can ever have this exact same person again, just in a different physical form—I don't think that's how human beings work. To be honest, I think I would be terrified at the sight of a dead loved one showing up at my doorstep several years later and going, "Hey, remember me?"

But I can see why reincarnation would be a comfort to a lot of people. My family, for instance, thinks that I am my dead uncle reincarnated. I can never relay that tidbit of information without laughing; I once used it in a game of Two Truths and a Lie with Toothpick and he asked, "Wait, what does that even mean?" Even after all these years, it still sounds absurd to me, although I guess death, especially the sudden death of a young person, is in itself quite absurd.

The Myanmar new year takes place in April and is known as Thingyan, or the Water Festival. The celebration lasts a week, during which most businesses are shut, and people walk and drive down the roads splashing water onto one another to signify fresh beginnings through the literal washing away of old sins and bad karma. To put it plainly, the whole country turns into one giant, carnivalesque water park. There is music and food and lots of singing and dancing and water—lots and lots, and lots, of water.

I've always hated Thingyan, partly because I (very logically, in my opinion) hate unsanitary streams of water being aimed at me. It's gross! You have to dress strategically before going out, but it doesn't matter because in the end, you're still soaked and shivering on the sidewalk while the Yangon sun shines down on you. The other reason is that I've always associated the time of year with Zan Lay, A May's youngest son and Mom's younger brother, who drowned when he was fourteen. In our family, that's more or less all Thingyan is and all it's ever been, at least since I was born—the time of year when Zan Lay died. I've known the story since I was a kid, but never in full detail, as is customary for all our family stories that are less than cheery.

From what I can piece together, Zan Lay and his friends were out walking along Kandawgyi Lake, near Karaweik, when he dropped a toy on a patch of dirt. He went over to the edge of the lake to wash his toy, but leaned in a bit too far, or possibly slipped on the mud and fell into the water, to the horror of his friends, none of whom knew how to swim. Very soon after, Ba Ba and his friends also happened to be walking through the same area. Zan Lay's friends ran over and told them what had happened, and Ba Ba and his friends dove into the lake to look for Zan Lay. It was Ba Ba who located Zan Lay and carried his unconscious body up to the surface. The roads were either closed off or deadlocked as they always are in Thingyan, and so Ba Ba, who couldn't have been more than eighteen or nineteen at the time, carried Zan Lay in his arms as the whole group ran to the hospital. Zan Lay was pronounced dead on arrival. This is the story I know.

There's that saying that things come in threes: Zan Lay's death came first, soon followed by the end of my grandparents' marriage; Mom always tells the two stories together, and I imagine they are linked in her own recollection, *x* leading to *y*. My grandfather and A May got divorced, and with her two oldest children married and living their own lives, A May moved in with my parents and became bored, as Mom tells me. With my father in the army and my mother working full-time,

A May didn't have much to do during the day apart from some housework and catching up with neighbors, and cooking dinner for two each night. Worried that her mother sat alone grieving in the house while she was at work five days a week, Mom decided soon after that this would be a good time for her and my dad to start trying for a child, mainly so that my grandmother would have something to do.

I was born on September 8, 1995, approximately a year and a half after my uncle died. But that wasn't when I first came into our family. The other story in our family is that one night, Zan Lay visited A May's sister Ma Gyi in a dream and told her that he had hit his head on a rock when he fell into the lake, and that was why he couldn't swim back up; he also told her not to worry because he'd be coming back to them soon. A few weeks after the dream, my mom announced that she was pregnant with me. Mom swears she hadn't told anyone that she and my dad had started trying, and Ma Gyi hadn't told anyone about her dream.

I grew up hearing about Zan Lay, and more specifically, about how *eerily* alike we were. He and I had the same chubby body. I had the same mole as him, except on the opposite cheek ("I think God made a mistake with the mole placement," Mom would joke). I had the same giggle as him when Mom tickled me in the same spot. We were both smart. We had the same hair texture and shy smile. And, of course, we both called my grandma A May. As far as my family was concerned, I was him reincarnated.

Unfortunately for my family, who developed a near-collective aquaphobia following this tragedy, I turned out to be a person who loves water. I love swimming in the rain, water engulfing me from below and above and at all sides, the feel of the drops on the back of my body from head to toe while the front is submerged in the deep blue pool. At the beach, I always wondered how far out I could swim (I bet I could swim pretty far, way further out past the little white ropes that tell you to stop). I never liked going to the pool with my friends because they wanted to play and have water fights, while I viewed the pool as a quiet, sacred place where all you should be doing was swimming. One time, I came to the pool with a friend's family, and the manager who always hung around said to my friend's parents, "Oh yeah, she comes here with her family all the time. She's a very good swimmer." I was so proud. "I am a very good swimmer," I tell people even now, even though I only go to the pool or the beach once or twice a year. But I *am* a good swimmer, I know I am. I never learned how to properly ride a bike—I wobble for the first few minutes and I'm bad at turning corners—but learning how to swim well was my equivalent; I could never forget. I could also never quite wrap my head around this deep-rooted fear of water that was held by everyone in my family, or at least every elder who could remember Zan Lay's death. Water is fascinating to me. When people ask me what I wanted to be when I was a kid, I say, "Mermaid, and then detective, and then writer." But mermaid always came first.

In spite of my finesse in the water, A May's aquaphobia was, and remains, the worst out of everybody's. We don't talk about why she's hesitant to let us go to the beach or a water park without her, or why in spite of her fears, she insisted that I learn to swim as early as possible. A May is strong and fearless; once, when she went to a clinic, and the doctor had to perform minor surgery on the spot and asked if she was scared, she replied, "No, I've been through worse. This is nothing." But she's terrified of any of her grandchildren being around water. "You know why" was my mother's answer whenever we pouted about everyone else getting to go to a birthday pool party or on a class field trip to Inle Lake.

But you can't ever fully avoid water. After all, some people even *choose* to bring life into the world via a pool of water; arguments in favor of water births maintain that it's the least traumatic way for a baby to be born because it replicates the conditions of an amniotic sac. I'm not a philosophical person, but I've always loved the thought of life being like an ocean wave, and when the wave inevitably crashes, the water returns to the sea; it brings me peace to think not that the water took Zan Lay away, but that he simply returned to the sea. And around the time I turned thirteen, I found myself picturing my life as a wave more and more often, and all *I* wanted to do was return to the sea, too.

It took me nearly half a year to suspect that something was wrong. I was about halfway through ninth grade when I realized that I had spent every night of the last five months crying myself to sleep. I don't know if it was the stress of high school and having teachers and counselors and parents drilling it in me that everything I did from now on would determine whether or not I would have a bright future, or if it was just teenage hormones. I didn't worry too much during the first few nights or even weeks, but then the weeks turned into every single week, which turned into months, and I still wasn't out of tears. I had a rough idea of what Mental Illness was, and at some point I had to admit to myself, as confusedly and warily as a thirteen-year-old could, that maybe there was something bigger going on than my being an emotional person. I was fine during the day—I looked forward to school where I had a core group of best friends, my grades were good, I was on the softball team, and I took part in the school musicals. At home, I had close, loving relationships with my parents and my siblings. And yet, toward the end of dinner each night, I would look forward to going to bed, to crawling under my duvet and turning off all the lights apart from the single night-light at the other end of the room, and letting something out—I didn't know what—as I sobbed and screamed into my pillow.

I didn't ever put myself in harm's way, but I knew that if I were to end up in a potentially dangerous situation like Zan Lay's, I probably wouldn't do anything about it. Some nights I wouldn't cry, but instead I'd close my eyes and, while holding my breath and staying as still as I could under the blanket, let my mind go blank, and I could almost pretend that I'd stopped existing. It took me a long time to learn that there is a term for this: *suicidal ideation*. I am not an idler by nature, but maybe if I idled for long enough in the right moment, I would get to die. In the water, you have to kick to keep moving. Maybe if I just ignored the instinct to kick for long enough, physics and biology would take over and my body would stop fighting and eventually hit the bottom of the lake. If you dive deep enough into the ocean, it becomes pitch-dark and you don't know which way is up or down; that was what I wanted—to sink to the ocean floor, somewhere in that 95 percent that still hasn't been explored.

It feels almost too poetic to say that I started to become depressed around the same age that Zan Lay drowned. Maybe a psychologist would posit that there was an awareness of my own mortality, which loomed closer as I approached the age he was when he died. The day I turned fifteen and officially outlived my uncle was probably one of the happiest days of A May's life. To my family, if I survived that year, they had accomplished their goal.

In the United States, Asian Americans are three times less likely than their white counterparts to seek mental health services. When I considered seeing a therapist in Yangon, I didn't even know where to start or whom to ask. I found an article that stated that the suicide mortality rate for Myanmar girls and women is approximately 9.5 deaths per 100,000 people, compared to the 7.7 global average. And, of course, there was the stigma and the accompanying fear of how this would reflect on my family. Even when I objectively knew that what I was struggling with wasn't wrong or shameful, I also knew that a lot of people would disagree. I knew that my mother would view it as a personal failure on her part, and that no matter how much I tried to explain that it was an actual illness and that there was something wrong with my brain, she'd feel that she could've prevented it; the worst part was that I knew that others would think the same of her.

My mom is one of my best friends, pretty much always has been, and I know I can talk to her about everything. She tells us so herself all the time, reminding us, "You know you can talk to me about anything" any time one of us is quiet and moody or lashing out but insists that there's nothing bothering us. But in my teenage mind, there were a handful of topics you just didn't approach, death and mental health being two of them, and for the first decade and a half of my life, you didn't talk about water or drowning either. You just didn't. And yet, every night, all three of these topics would swirl around in my head, and it would feel, as the apt saying goes, as though I was drowning in my thoughts.

I've come close to drowning once in my life. It happened years before any swimming lessons, while I was playing in the pool with my dad and siblings and I decided that I wanted to know what drowning felt like, not in a suicidal way, but as though I wanted to try wine for the first time. I paddled over to a section of the pool where I couldn't reach the bottom, removed my inflatable floaties, and instinct kicked in and my arms and legs flapped around in desperation. Dad didn't notice because he was sorting out something for Shan, and a lifeguard who spotted me had to jump in and save me. I'm the kind of person who would rather bleed to death than inconvenience a stranger and call out for help if I was getting stabbed on the street, but that day, when I realized that I could actually fucking die right there in the pool and ruin all of these families' weekends, I screamed as loud as I could while flapping for my life.

When I used to swim in the shallow end of the pool as a kid, I'd hold my breath as long as possible and reach for the fake rocks underwater, pretending to be a mermaid. In an essay for *The Outline*, the writer Anna Borges compares suicidal ideation to constantly treading water so that you don't drown in the middle of an ocean; I could—can—empathize with this so well, although, unlike Borges, it didn't occur to me for a long time that humans aren't supposed to live in the water, that you're not supposed to always be trying to stay afloat on this spectrum between actively wanting to drown and fantasizing about what it'd be like to drown. At some point, the water became all I ever knew, and it took me until my early twenties to realize that I sort of missed the land, and I wondered if anyone had even noticed I was out at sea.

When I became old enough to wonder out loud why all my friends got to go to the pool and I didn't, my family was faced with a conundrum: How do you conquer a fear that you refuse to acknowledge? I remember being so excited when my parents took me to my first one-on-one swimming lesson, but as soon as the instructor led me to the pool, I burst into tears and screamed at the top of my lungs until Dad picked me up and assured me that we were going home. But a few years later, when we tried swimming lessons again, and this time with Phyo and Shan as well, I begged my parents for fifteen more minutes at the end of each of our sessions. Maybe it was because my brother and sister, who were too young to really understand the concept of the reincarnation story and hadn't grown up constantly being reminded of it, turned the pool into a site of fun. Maybe I was tired of being excluded from my friends' pool parties. Or maybe, unfortunately for my parents and grandparents, that was my first-ever real act of rebellion against them, like when I drop a piece of food on the floor and Mom specifically tells me *not* to eat it, and so of course I must proceed to maintain direct eye contact as I put the scrap in my mouth. Whether I was Zan Lay or not, I felt determined to become good at swimming, and comfortable in and around water, so as to break this chain of fear that had run through my family. When it came to my own mental health, too, as scary and difficult as it was to research and speak up about what was going on in my brain, I knew I had to, or else even if water didn't kill me, these thoughts very possibly could. It turns out that sometimes literally all you need to do is yell for help and people will come to your rescue, like the lifeguard did that one time. When, at last, I confided in people that I needed help from time to time, no one told me I had no right to be depressed or to want to die; all they wanted to do was listen and help, and they did.

It turns out that so much of life, in addition to reincarnation, is cyclical. Stigma and guilt, for instance; and with that, also shame. A calendar. Or the water cycle. So is fear—fear of water leads to a fear of swimming leads to a fear of water. But some cycles are meant to be broken.

For a long time, I wasn't sure that I would ever reach a point where I was comfortable talking or just writing about these topics—water, drowning, death, suicidal ideation—and sharing it with a wider group of people. I'd marvel at my friends who mentioned in passing that they saw therapists on a regular basis, or that they were on antidepressants, or even that they'd survived past suicide attempts. The thing was, though, when one of them brought up something like this and they did so not as though it was this huge secret or source of deep shame, it gave me that little push to confide in them as well, and then, suddenly, I didn't feel so alone and as though I was all by myself out in the middle of the ocean anymore. You take swimming lessons because you *want* to know how to swim, even if it may take you weeks or months or perhaps years to get the hang of things. For my first few swimming lessons, all I was instructed to do was hold on to the edge of the pool with my hands and keep kicking my legs behind me until I was confident about letting go. "Just keep paddling," the teacher would repeat. I would look around at the other people in the pool—kids and adults—who were jumping off the diving board and swimming about without any floaties, and he'd recenter my focus to my paddling. I didn't need to worry about them, he said. I'd be swimming just like them soon. But for now, I could hold on to that ledge for as long as I needed to before I wanted to try letting go.

Years ago, we went on a large family vacation to Ngwe Saung Beach. I was surprised Mom and A May finally agreed because Ngwe Saung is notorious for its strong tides. We always went to Chaung Thar instead when we were children, but that year, Mom and A May decided that we should visit Ngwe Saung at least once. A May had an artificial knee, and it was dangerous for her to go into the water on the beach, so Mom splurged on getting us a fancy villaesque situation at a hotel, complete with a private swimming pool in the middle of our bungalows. On our first evening, A May ventured into the pool—the first time I'd ever seen her do that. "Hold on to my hand, don't let me go," she kept repeating to her sister and nephew as she sat down on the edge of the pool and then slowly sank her body into the water, which came up to about halfway up her chest. Then, still holding on to them, she left the wall to walk toward the center of the pool, a hesitant but growing smile on her face. She went in several times a day for the rest of the trip, and even when most of us ran down to the beach and played in the waves, she'd be content floating in the pool with her eyes closed, just soaking in the water for as long as she could. We were all shocked at how much she loved it, though I think *she* was the most surprised. Several months later, when Mom proposed the idea of going back to that beach, or just any beach, A May said, "Yes. We should do that again."

A BAKING ESSAY I NEED TO WRITE

When I was in graduate school in London, there was a woman on my course who was around my age, and who was kind and smart and gorgeous, with perfect shiny blond hair and sparkling blue eyes. She also worked at a pastry shop, and loved to bake in her spare time. Our overall cohort was divided up into two classes, and we were in the morning class, which started at 9:00 a.m.; on more than one occasion, and while the rest of us straggled in with a hastily purchased cup of coffee from the Caffè Nero across from our classroom building, this woman would cheerily present a plate of cookies or cupcakes and pass it around the class, adding, "I woke up early and couldn't go back to sleep so I baked this" in a very casual tone that I would've found overbearing or braggy had it not been for the fact that she was a very nice person. It's safe to say that I was jealous of her—not just because she was that infuriating mixture of good looks and a sweet disposition, but because a part of me had always wanted to be the kind of person who brought freshly baked goods to a group meeting and said as I tossed my hair over my shoulder in a nonchalant manner, "I hope these are good, I just whipped them up this morning" when I knew full well that the goods I was presenting were fucking great.

My very first time baking anything was during my sophomore year of college when, bored one afternoon, my friend Noah and I went to the Dollar Tree in town and got a box of Betty Crocker Chocolate Chip Cookie Mix, along with measuring cups, baking sheet, whisk, parchment paper, and whatever else the box said we would need. The end product was disgusting, and while neither of us were arrogant enough to declare that it wasn't because *we'd* messed up, we also figured that we got pretty much what was expected from a boxed mix from Dollar Tree.

I did not start properly baking again until several years later when I was in my early twenties. A Myanmar American family friend was visiting Yangon for the first time since her family had left the country when she was a child, and I offered her the spare room in my apartment. She had a culinary background, and in exchange for my letting her stay for free, she promised to teach me how to bake. In the weeks leading up to her trip, she would email me asking what items I wanted to bake, and arrived in Yangon with a small stash of vanilla extract, chocolate chips, and a few other ingredients that she worried we might not be able to procure here. On one of our first days, we went to the biggest baking supply shop in the city and she guided me in picking out spatulas, palette knives, parchment paper, baking trays, a pastry brush, and a box of assorted piping tips. We printed out several recipes that she'd gathered (she insisted on doing things the old-fashioned way and having the instructions on a physical piece of paper), and I was in giddy awe every time we poured batter into cupcake tins or turned dark brown bananas into a loaf of sweet, moist banana bread. I kept baking even after she left, pushing myself to try new, more complicated recipes each time, and beaming every time they came out perfectly. It soon became my *thing*, for better or for worse. My family stopped buying birthday cakes, instead flattering their way into having me bake a cake for every party, and I still fall for it every time like a damn fool.

I've wanted to write a personal reflective piece about baking for many years now, but always hesitate at how absurd that might seem—a Myanmar person writing an essay about baking cookies and cakes? The closest Myanmar cuisine has to a cake is sanwin makin, which is actually a variation of the Indian suji ka halwa, and still isn't actually a cake. I used to wonder why it was that no auntie or grandma I knew, even outside of my own family, was really a baker, despite so many of them being great cooks. The first and last time I opened the oven in my parents' kitchen, I discovered giant spiderwebs inside; when I screamed at A May, she bent over and peered at it, and then shrugged and said, "I don't even know what that's for" (by *that*, she meant the entire oven that was right underneath her five burners). To satisfy my own unique curiosity, I spent a few nights googling "myanmar baking culture" or "burmese baking" or "baking burmese myanmar food," but all I got was a list of baking supply shops in the country. Finally, when COVID-19 hit and my local social media feeds were overtaken by photos of cookies and croissants and red velvet cakes, I decided to answer my own question and successfully pitched an article looking at the role of baking and baked desserts in Myanmar cuisine.

I found out that one of the main reasons baking isn't a part of our culture is because it often requires dairy products—butter, cream, cheese, milk chocolate—that in turn require a fridge, which in turn requires reliable electricity (which anyone who's lived in Myanmar will tell you is not a given, even at the best of times, and in the richest of neighborhoods). In her fantastic cookbook *Mandalay*, my friend MiMi Aye has a section titled "Equipment in the Burmese Kitchen," and ovens, whisks, and spatulas, rightfully, do not make the list. A cleaver, a chopper, and a cook's knife each do, because, all in all, we are a cooking culture, and we take our different knives very seriously! And in place of dairy, Myanmar cuisine leans on dried ingredients, which have long shelf lives and can be stored in a cabinet for several months as A May's array of reused empty mayonnaise and jam jars in our dining room cabinet has demonstrated for decades. The weather in the tropics also actively works against you when you are baking. You're supposed to work dough with your fingertips because those are the coolest parts of your hand, but that doesn't matter when you're working in a kitchen that's at 30°C to begin with.

The whole time I was working on this "baking in Myanmar" article, I became increasingly aware that culturally, socioeconomically, geographically speaking, I'm not meant to be interested in baking—except I am, aren't I? When a friend calls me and asks why their recipe didn't turn out well, and they talk through the steps they took, I can almost always pinpoint where they went wrong. When someone who wants to get into baking asks me what common mistakes they should remember, I tell them:

- Always sift your dry ingredients. Yes, it's a pain in the ass, but what is an even bigger pain is getting a giant clump of baking soda in a bite of cake.
- Fold your brownie batter with a spatula, never with a mixer. The same goes for banana bread.
- Crack eggs into a separate bowl first before

putting them into your batter so that you're not suddenly elbow-deep in your mixing bowl trying to locate a single stray eggshell.

- Don't forget to poke holes at both ends of your éclairs as soon as they're out of the oven; this will let the steam escape and stop the insides from getting soggy.
- The microwave can bring almost any ingredient to room temperature in a matter of seconds.

And so much more. I know now how to bake the way A May knows how to cook—which is to say, intuitively. I cannot whip up three different curries in under half an hour like A May, but I know I can now show up to a 9:00 a.m. class with a perfect platter of fudgy brownies.

My teal KitchenAid stand mixer is my pride and joy. I joke—but only partly—that if there was ever an emergency, and if I knew my dogs and my passport had already made it out safely, my mixer would be the one thing I'd grab and run with. I'd lusted after a KitchenAid stand mixer ever since the first time I saw a professional chef use one, which was probably on some episode of *MasterChef*. Over the years, I'd spot it on TV, or on the kitchen counters of famous chefs' Instagram photos and house tours, or in the background on cookbook covers. So when Mom and I were in a shopping center, and after she watched me gaze longingly at the rows of colored mixers at the KitchenAid stall and then told me to pick one, I couldn't even pretend to not want it. "It's my present. You bake all the time, so I know you'll put it to good use," she told me. I squealed when I unboxed it in my kitchen, and now it sits in the middle of my island to tell everyone who walks in: "Yes, I am a Real Baker. In fact, I do so much baking that I require this highly regarded piece of machinery to do all of my mixing and whisking for me." One *Eater* article referring to the mixer as an "icon" calls it "a countertop staple for any home baker worth their salt and a colorful kitchen showpiece for plenty who aren't." When I posted a photo of my new prized possession on social media, I gleefully watched as several friends responded with heart-eyes emojis and many, many exclamation marks. But when I came home that evening with my teal mixer in tow, Mom nodded at it and had to explain to A May, "It's for baking. It was very expensive"; I think A May smiled and said something along the lines of "It's . . . very nice."

In Myanmar homes, the ultimate countertop staple (or stovetop staple, in our case) is a set of dan ohs, which MiMi accurately refers to in her book as "universal cooking pots." I've learned that in a lot of American families, their KitchenAid is viewed as a prized heirloom that forges strong emotional bonds as it gets passed down through generations; when I moved into my own place, A May insisted on gifting me with my own set of stackable, multiple-sized dan ohs, telling me how the ones we have at the house have been in her possession for decades. And despite owning what seems to me like more dan ohs than any one person could possibly need in a single lifetime, A May always seems to be running out of dan ohs while she's cooking multiple curries; I, on the other hand, am always frantically washing a mixing bowl or whisk in between starting a new batter. I do not understand the appeal or functionality of these handle-less aluminum pots, but A May and my aunties don't understand why Mom paid the equivalent of several hundred thousand kyats for a heavy teal machine that needs to be treated with the utmost care and requires a separate fabric cover.

I still sometimes feel strange referring to myself as a baker (even if just a home baker) instead of just someone who likes to bake, not dissimilar to when I was younger and the idea of calling myself a writer felt scary and weird and, to an extent, wrong. I did not think young girls who had names like mine were allowed to call themselves writers, especially in white spaces, and I did not know how someone raised on Myanmar curries and, in general, a cuisine that has very few, if any, traces of oven culture, could be called a baker. Two of my top baking recipe sites, *Sally's Baking Addiction* and *Laura in the Kitchen*, are run by beaming white women who obviously also own

KitchenAid mixers and who have baking in their blood. "As a young girl, I spent hours watching my mother and grandmother work their baking magic . . . By the time I picked up my first mixing spoon, I was hooked." writes Sally McKenney on her website's "About" page. But when I couldn't figure out why bits of my cupcakes tasted extremely salty, I didn't have a baking connoisseur grandmother or aunt to turn to, and instead had to rely on years-old online baking forum threads (which was where and how I learned the sifting tip).

Obviously, baked pastries are not an entirely white and/or European field, nor do they solely belong to these groups. Every January or February, depending on the calendar year, we gleefully accept boxes of mooncakes from Chinese friends celebrating the Lunar New Year. You haven't lived until you've tried milk bread, and no one can convince me otherwise. When Khin and I lived in London, we would often get dinner at the Four Seasons in Chinatown, and then count our change as we let our noses lead the way toward the bustling taiyaki store around the corner where we would *each* gleefully buy a bag of six golden fish that would burn our tongues because we were too impatient to heed the chef's warning to "be careful, very hot!" But in spite of this giant world of baked delights that exists beyond cheery white women's intentionally rustic kitchens, you still get instances such as *The Great British Bake Off*'s catastrophic "Japanese

Week" of Season 11 that suggests to viewers that, even now, baking is still largely viewed and approached through a Eurocentric lens. For this particular challenge, one contestant sprinkled matcha powder on top of their mille crêpes cake and presented it as having fulfilled the directive; another made Chinese pork floss buns, because Asian is Asian, right? It reminded me of the number of online recipes for tropical baked desserts that I've encountered that have ended in me wanting to furiously comment, "This isn't a *tropical* cookie just because it has coconut!" or "Canned mangoes on top of a slice of chiffon cake does not make it *tropical*!!!" Brigitte Malivert, a Black pastry chef who studied in Paris, explained in her *Eater* essay "Layers of Obstruction" that in French pastry school, tropical flavors such as mango, passion fruit, and coconut are always referred to as "exotique"; chocolate, vanilla, and coffee are not, even though neither mangoes nor vanilla are native French ingredients. Whenever someone on *MasterChef* or *The Great British Bake Off* makes something that wouldn't traditionally be consumed in a European household, their creation is frequently labeled as *exotic* (or *exotique*) or *innovative*, because the norm is always European.

I don't think of myself as being a serious enough chef to have a culinary idol, but if I had to pick one, it would undoubtedly be Christina Tosi: the green-eyed, blond-haired founder of Momofuku Milk Bar. It's always been a bucket list dream of mine to try Momofuku's birthday cake, and I've become even more desperate since I found out that Jay-Z raved about it at Taylor Swift's twenty-fifth birthday party. But then there is the part of me that feels like the fact that my culinary dream is to eat, and maybe one day even try to replicate, this random white woman's cake makes me a bad Brown person. One particular food experience that I've repeatedly encountered in food writing by writers of color living in the West—such as Geeta Kothari's essay in which she explores the titular question "If You Are What You Eat, Then What Am I?" or Brigid Washington's ode to callaloo in "This Simple, Soulful Dish Tells the Story of My Ancestors," or Alexis Watts's "I've Never Felt Truly Mexican, But Cooking with My Mom Helps"—is an individual's decision to solidify their cultural roots by mastering the cuisine of their homeland, or by teaching their own children the complex history behind a specific dish or recipe that the latter might initially reject just as *they* once did (and sometimes in the process, the writer unloads decades of internalized shame and/or discovers new aspects of their identity that were previously unexplored). MiMi herself writes in the introduction to *Mandalay*: "My folks, especially my mother, had a deathly fear that I would somehow end up rejecting my 'Burmeseness' [in England] so, in order to instil a 'proper' sense of culture, they taught me the beautiful Burmese language with its winsome and bubble-like script, raised us as strict-ish Buddhist and reared us on brilliant Burmese food." Because that's what food does—it makes and maintains connections beyond the kitchen and the dining table. Yet, when I was living in London or even in the Berkshires, and found myself craving la phet thoke or arloo htamin or falooda, I would either seek them out somewhere else—in London, it was at one of two Myanmar restaurants in the city, and in Great Barrington, Massachusetts, it was at the home of a Myanmar family friend who lived a few minutes' walk away—or shrug and say, "Oh well, I'll have it next time I go back home." When my white friends or partners' families jokingly asked me when I was going to treat them to a Myanmar meal, I would laugh and say, "Whenever you want to head into town, I know this great place." When I was living in Norwich and wanted to get into cooking, instead of poring over Myanmar recipes on the internet and triumphantly gathering all of the necessary ingredients at the Asian food stall in Norwich Market, I signed up for a HelloFresh subscription through which I made Italian, French, Indian, and Mexican foods, but never Myanmar; and I was okay with that. I loved the mere act of cooking in the same kitchen as Toothpick, never really paying attention to the food or cuisine that we were actually making.

Maybe I should have been—should still be—more

embarrassed about the fact that I need to refer to a cook-book to cook a Myanmar dish, but try as I might (and I've tried really hard), I can't find it in myself to feel this way. After all, god forbid a Brown person does something purely for joy, with no backstory of shame or struggle attached. A food writer friend told me about how she was once approached by a big food magazine to write a short love letter to her favorite ingredient, and she chose wholegrain mustard. Then she was almost surprised that they *let* her write about her affinity for mustard because, well, it was essentially a fluff piece, and, as she put it so perfectly, "They come to you to write about Asian stuff, but not fluff pieces." There is no shame or struggle in fluff.

I'm putting it out there now that no one should come to me to write about "Asian food," because I cannot cook Myanmar food by heart—this is a fact, and why should I feel embarrassed about a fact that I am, at best, indifferent toward? I know that last question is a rhetor-ical one because I am already well aware of why I should feel embarrassed. This is how the conversation plays out in my head:

> **Voice 1:** Why do you think an Oreo cheesecake is *better* than, say, kyet u hin?
>
> **Voice 2:** No, I don't think it's *better*! I love kyet u hin! I'm just not interested in cooking it myself.
>
> **Voice 1:** But why not?

Voice 2: Because it's boring—

Voice 1: Why is it boring? Because it's not white?

Voice 2: No, because it's ... I dunno ... boring.
Like ... science. Or math. It's not fun—

Voice 1: Oh, so your own cuisine, your entire heritage, is *boring* and *not fun*, is it?

Voice 2: No, that's not what I—

I've had this debate with nobody but myself, but oftentimes, it's your own internalized guilt that is the most distressing. It would be one thing if I had zero interest in the kitchen whatsoever; "Pyae's signature meal is takeout," Mom and A May always joke with friends who ask if I've picked up any of my grandmother's signature recipes, and I roll my eyes but nod in agreement. But the reality is that I would spend all day in the kitchen baking my cupcakes and brownies and tarts if I could, and that I do have a signature meal that isn't a Myanmar dish, but a tray of the most perfect red velvet cheesecake brownies. It's strange to feel guilty about not feeling guilty, about *not* wanting to shout, "Fuck your Western desserts! Who needs macarons when you have curries and fresh mangoes!" because the truth is, as much as I love curries and mangoes, *I* still want macarons.

I always thought that if and when I wrote an essay about baking, it would be about how my passion for baking is at odds with my grandmother's passion for cooking (she's the chef of our house), and how that culinary difference speaks to a wider cultural gap between us. I found a draft that I started a few years ago that opened with how I took up baking to help myself, the Brown girl, better assimilate into new white, Western environments.

I'm not saying that what I wrote is a lie; from experience, I will tell you that it does help to break the ice at a dinner party in a white household if you show up with a platter of brownies. Everything Malivert wrote remains true; there is systemic racism present in almost every aspect of the professional culinary world, including in the pastry sphere. Non-Western cooks are expected to perfect Western recipes and techniques in order to be a *real* chef or baker, but Western, and often white, cooks are allowed to modernize and experiment to produce "fusion" food (which is a *scam*, in my opinion). White chefs provide the templates as well as the final grades, and while one lot is praised for thinking outside the box, the other is penalized for even slightly straying from the directive. I know if I ever pursued baking as an actual career, and especially if I tried to do so in a Western environment, then my name and skin color and country of birth would mean I had so much more to prove before I even rolled out my first croissant.

The more I find myself navigating primarily white spaces—in college, in the workplace, in the homes of friends and partners' families—the more I feel a sense of almost needing to assimilate according to the narrative of guilt, or at least of struggle, that so many of them seem to assume is mine. I must have some story about cooking my grandmother's signature dish in my London apartment and having neighbors complain about the stinky smell coming out of my window, or one about going along with my primarily white group of friends to places like Shake Shack and Five Guys when all I craved was a meal at a Myanmar restaurant, or about how I got into baking as my own small way of rebelling against my otherwise strictly traditional Myanmar upbringing. They assume I must constantly feel as though I'm being pulled between two cultures—and I often do, but not when it comes to baking.

In her essay "The Limits of the Lunchbox Moment," Jaya Saxena dissects the lunchbox moment trope that is present in so many pieces of art such as personal essays and standup routines by people of color; everyone knows it by now—the moment when a child who isn't white opens their lunchbox at school and is ridiculed by their white classmates for bringing weird or stinky food. However, Saxena interviews various people of color who did *not* experience the lunchbox moment growing up, and reflects on the desire to belong as a person of color, and how "so much of belonging for people in marginalized groups has to do with shared struggle"; the article asks the question that if the lunchbox moment is almost a rite of passage for any non-white child growing up in a predominantly white country, what does it say or mean if you *didn't* experience that? I'm not denying that there are a lot of things about my upbringing and heritage that I've glazed over or actively shunned as a result of internalized racism or Eurocentrism, but cooking isn't one of them. I don't cook any particular cuisine, including Myanmar, because I have no interest in cooking. I pursued a degree and career in the arts over one in STEM because I just wasn't interested in math; sometimes white friends or colleagues ask me if my parents ever vehemently tried to talk me out of being a writer, and my answer is always "No, my mother has always been, and remains, my embarrassingly loudest cheerleader." I cannot relate to the many people of color out there who unfortunately *have* been shamed into being embarrassed about their culinary upbringings and tried to replace their heritage with one that was more palatable in a Western context, but I'm trying to remind myself that that is okay, and that I do not, and will not, share the same experiences as every other non-white, non-Western baker in the world. Instead, I've found shared experiences in bakers like *MasterChef Australia*'s renowned dessert king Reynold Poernomo, and *British Bake Off* queen Nadiya Hussain, who was entrusted with baking Queen Elizabeth's birthday cake, and Trang Doan, whose "About" page on *Wild Wild Whisk* doesn't talk about having grown up wistfully watching her mother and grandmother bake, but does feature a very familiar story of how she grew up in "an apartment with an oven and a dishwasher that my mom used as extra storage for pots and pans"—all of these bakers who happen to be people of color but who also started baking not because there was some deeply held sense of self-hatred or desire to assimilate, but because, well, baking is so fucking *fun*.

I take great pride in my chewy brownies. I bake because I love to bake. I love baking because of its precision—something that any Myanmar person will tell you is absent in our way of cooking, which encourages eyeballing over following actual recipes. I like measuring spoons and cups and exact temperatures; A May likes winging things and tasting as she goes along. Sometimes you just like the things you like because you like them. Some gaps in personal interests are never meant to be bridged.

The only reason Noah and I made that trip to the Dollar Tree and split fifteen dollars between us was because we had nothing better to do that afternoon and wanted to have fun; if he, a white American dude, doesn't have to have a deeper undercurrent of struggle behind that afternoon, why should I? I thought that if and when I ever wrote an essay like this, it would be about how my baking journey has led to some serious soul-searching—and it is, but not in the ways that for so long I forced myself to believe it would. These days, I bake because it brings me joy and because I am good at it, and the more I do it and the more I challenge myself, the better I get and the happier I am. When one of my best friends started baking for the first time in quarantine during the COVID-19 pandemic, I was excited to share tips and tricks and ingredients with her, putting a metaphorical arm around her shoulder from six feet away and introducing her to this magical space where the need for concentrated precision distracts you from whatever is happening beyond your kitchen walls, even if only for a few hours. After all, how wonderful it is when Brown people operating in white spaces still manage to carve out and welcome others into our happy place, exotique ingredients and all.

UNIQUE SELLING POINT

When I tell people that I'm a writer, and a non-fiction one at that, one of the first things they ask me is what I write about, to which I gesture at the air with both hands and say, "Everything, really." The main reason I was drawn to nonfiction from a young age was, frankly, because of my nosiness. My favorite class I took during my undergraduate years was a personal essay writing workshop, and my favorite part of the class would be when everyone's essays would appear in my inbox twice a week, and I'd get a firsthand account of my fellow classmates' lives. Our professor had told us from the first day that everything that was shared in the class would not and could not go beyond those four walls, and because it was a small group, and a good one, we let ourselves be surprisingly vulnerable about every aspect of our lives, from first kisses to medical histories to travelogues. The one exception, though, the one topic I absolutely, positively refused to write about because I would-rather-chew-off-my-right-arm-and-then-my-left-if-I-had-to hate writing about, was Race (open air quotes, capital *R*, close air quotes).

I had a privileged but generally average, by all accounts, upbringing. My dad was in the army, and my mom had an office job, and together with A May, we lived in a ground-floor apartment in a neighborhood downtown where the kids hung out on the sidewalk while our uncles played chin lone or soccer in the middle of the street. My parents saved up money, and right before my brother was born, we moved to the suburbs and into a larger, nicer two-story house with a colorful garden that remains A May's pride and joy. I am the oldest of three children; my brother and my sister are assholes but also the only human beings on whose behalf I would murder someone.

I thrive on being an introvert, but I like to think that I'm still an interesting-enough individual to hold my own in conversation at a party, so I always seethe when anyone, but especially a white person, gives me a quick glance up and down and I know they're wondering if they should ask *the* question. I've only been on a handful of first dates in my life, but every time, the guy's eyes have lit up and they've sat up a bit straighter in their chair when they do finally ask me and I answer that I'm from Myanmar "or Burma, if that's what you know it as." It doesn't matter that I have a whole list of interests and anecdotes that I'd rather talk about—I'm well read in nineteenth-century French literature, I've watched almost every post-2002 East Asian horror film and even wrote a whole dissertation on horror films in translation, I once ran into Malala Yousafzai in the bathroom—because all they want to know once we've placed our order is "So, Burma. What was it like growing up there?" They've always wanted to go to Thailand or Indonesia, they tell me, but they know almost nothing about Burma. It's so exotic, so different, so cool. I don't think something's cool just because you haven't heard of it before, but first dates, chatty Uber drivers, tour guides—they all think it's so cool that I'm from Myanmar, they tell me I'm the first person from there that they've ever met! In writing workshops, I focus all my energy on not letting my eyes roll into the back of my head whenever someone comments about how they "would love to see more of your background, where you grew up, you know?" *No*, I think. *I don't* actually know, *Miranda*.

I used to love writing about white people whenever I wrote fiction. It became clear early on in all the pieces I workshopped in the few fiction classes I've taken that my own characters, the ones I'd conjured up with my ten brown fingers, were all Caucasian. They had names like Isabella and Tom, and grew up in predominantly white suburban neighborhoods in London and New York and

Québec. Once I embraced that there was no requirement for fidelity in fiction, I went wild with the white references in my stories—smooth, flawless porcelain skin (I loved giving my white characters porcelain skin), big blue eyes the size of the Atlantic Ocean, a family who wore shoes indoors with children who could snap at their parents without fear of permanent exile. And if anyone questioned why my writing was so white, I could feign shock and say with a laugh, "I guess I was just subconsciously influenced by Western media and publishing trends, you know?"—which we all know promote and favor art that centers white people. "Did you know," I could proffer, "a 2018 study showed that seventy-seven percent of characters depicted in children's books were white or animals and objects, while only seven percent were Asian or Pacific Islander? Incomprehensible, right?" I need to pay the bills, and to pay the bills I need my books to sell, and to sell books I *need* to write books about white characters (or I guess, alternatively, toys that come to life). The best, most comforting lies are those backed up by logic and statistics.

In contrast, in my nonfiction classes, where I was encouraged to write *the truth*, and hyper-focused on doing so, I'd always feel so guilty whenever I submitted yet another piece about my very Brown, very non-Western life for workshopping to all the other students, most of whom, if not all, were white. *We get it*, I imagined them saying over coffee as they rolled their eyes at the sight of another email from me. *You're Myanmar, you don't have to keep rubbing it in our faces.* Sometimes I daydream about writing just fiction. I love writing non-fiction, but I do want to write fiction professionally at some point in my career, if for no other reason than so that I can write a single five-thousand-word piece without once ever mentioning the words "Myanmar" or "Burma" or "Burmese"; this is a layered, twisted daydream, and I know I will never do this, but sometimes it's interesting to see where my daydreams lead. I used to read interviews with authors of color who wrote entire novels set in non-Western countries and featuring non-white characters, and they would almost always say something like "Well, growing up, I never saw books that had characters that looked like me, so I went ahead and wrote one"; and while I understood where they were coming from, as a young teen artist whose Brownness seemed to follow me around like a second shadow, being the Myanmar writer who voluntarily wrote a novel set in Myanmar and featuring Myanmar characters felt like an act of self-sabotage.

As I operated in more of these classes and workshops (and in general, just social spaces), it also began to occur to me that there was a distinction between being expected to write about Asianness and about Myanmarness. A lot of white classmates and teachers *knew* Asia and books by Asian writers from countries like China and Japan and India, but Myanmar singularly seemed to be exotic, interesting, mysterious. For all of Western media's lumping of every single Asian ethnicity under the general *Asian* umbrella, a white person's idea of Myanmar is usually very different from their idea of Tokyo or Singapore; in their imagination, the latter is bright and shiny and, essentially, *civilized*, while the former conjures up images of bamboo huts and dirt roads. When they asked to see more of my background, I knew they were asking for more bamboo huts. An American high school history teacher of mine told us that at one point, to the rest of the world, we were "like North Korea" in our enigmatism. It hit me that, as the lone mythical Myanmar unicorn in every writing space I attended, I was expected to write about Asia, yes, but more than that, to write about the mysterious country of Myanmar and our equally alien ways of life.

And so I came to realize that, perhaps, it wasn't necessarily, or at least not *just*, my race (Asian, or even Southeast Asian) that I was refusing to write about, but, specifically, my ethnicity (Myanmar). Whenever a South or East Asian artist received their share of the Hollywood spotlight, I couldn't pinpoint why I, an Asian person, still didn't feel as completely happy or represented as I should have at the sight of another successful Asian person. I used to say that I'd ideally have Mindy Kaling play me in my biopic, not only because I think she's hilarious and I love her as a writer and actress, but also because she was the only prolific dark-skinned American celebrity of South Asian descent whom I felt kind of, maybe, if you squinted and were a tiny bit racist, looked like me.

When I had my graduation ceremony for my associate degree, Mom was the only member of our family who could make it over to the United States. In the months leading up to her trip, we talked about what I would wear on the day. She was so excited—our whole family was—because apart from Mom herself, I was the first one in our extended family to have a graduation abroad, and the very first one to graduate in *America*, no less. In our conversations, I softly ventured that I wanted to splurge on a nice dress from Zara or J.Crew, but Mom remained adamant. "So what color hta mein do you want to wear? Do you think your measurements we took in December are still the same?" she asked during our video calls. There was never any question in her mind—I would be wearing a traditional Myanmar hta mein, obviously one made of silk, because this was a big occasion, and you only wear silk to big occasions. "Can you tell me your shoe size again? And do you want flat slippers or something higher?" she asked a few days before she went to Bogyoke Market to buy me a new pair of velvet slippers, which any Myanmar person knows are also the only appropriate choice of footwear for a special occasion. In the end, we compromised. Mom said I could wear anything I wanted *after* we had taken pictures.

The morning of the ceremony, we both got dressed in our formfitting short-sleeved yin bones and matching sleek hta meins at a friend's house near campus. When Mom dropped me off in front of the classrooms where I had to collect my cap and gown, my cheeks burned as I looked around at all the other girls in my class who were wearing the kinds of dresses that I had added to my online cart but never checked out. "Oh my god, your outfit is so pretty!" my roommate Megan said when she saw me waiting in line. I smiled and said, "Thank you," but I also knew that she was only saying it because it was a non-white outfit; I could've been wearing the tackiest, ugliest yin bone and hta mein set in the world, and she would've still felt the need to say that it looked great. When I got to the front of the line and they located my gown, I snatched it off the railing, slid my hands through the giant billowy black sleeves, and zipped it all the way up to the top. The bottom few inches of my hta mein, along with my matching velvet slippers, still peeked out from the bottom, and I hoped very hard that people would only look at me from the calf up. The yin bone still went up to my neck, though, and when friends saw a glimpse and asked what I was wearing, I tried to breezily say that it was "a traditional Myanmar outfit,"

because of course it was—that's what I was, in case anyone forgot. As soon as the ceremony was over and Mom
had made me pose for at least a hundred photos, I went
into the nearest bathroom, changed into a loose sum-
mery maxi dress, and felt a sigh of relief work its way
up from my velvet-slippered toes. I rejoined my friends
and teachers on the lawn, laughing and posing for photos and sliding in and out of conversations, and more
importantly, not having to deal with any more strangers
coming up to me and touching my shoulder and asking
me where I was from and what this beautiful outfit was
called; and every time someone did do that, my mind
drifted back to my then-boyfriend's dad asking me at
a lunch once, "That's a beautiful dress. Is that a traditional Burmese outfit?" and, both amused and confused,
I'd replied, "Umm, no, I got it at Forever 21."

I got so increasingly sick of people who read my
writing only ever asking me about "life in Myanmar" or
"Burmese culture" that at one point, young, stubborn
teenage me made a deal with myself that I wouldn't write
about my race or my ethnicity. Writing about my background was a cop-out; my white classmates and teachers would hesitate to say anything bad about my work
for fear of being branded a racist, even if what I had
written was actually bad. I knew I was a good writer,
and it made me so angry that I wasn't, however, a good
enough writer to write a whole piece without letting it

slip that I was Myanmar. But I couldn't exactly say my mother's name was Karen and that my dad was Bob and talk about our white picket fence house in the suburbs of Boston either. Still, though, I had to try. What bits I couldn't hide of my hta mein and yin bone in real life, I was determined to cover up in my writing. For a long time, my only creative goal was to have a stranger read my writing without once realizing that I wasn't white, and specifically, that I was Myanmar.

Instead of lying, I just left it all out—all the nuance and details and anecdotes about my life and the culture that shaped my view of the world. I would write out a paragraph and go back and delete every adjective or noun that gave away my background, like I was some PG-13 editor at a daytime television show whose job it was to bleep out every time a guest said "fuck" or "shit" or "asshole," except my job was to bleep out "Pyae" or "htamin" or "Yangon." I craved proof that I wasn't just the Myanmar girl who wrote about Myanmar stuff, or even Asian stuff, because my life was so much more than that. *I* was so much more than that. I think it's important to contextualize this by admitting that I didn't just do this for one assignment, or a few chapters of a hypothetical book—rather, I did this for several consecutive years. When you learn about craft, one of the first things you learn is the importance and distinctiveness of a writer's voice. I was certain that all *I* had when it came to *my* voice was that it was Myanmar, and I was desperate to change that. I wanted my voice to be funny, and unflinching, and thoughtful; I didn't believe that my voice could be all of those things as well as being Myanmar.

A professor told me that half the battle of editing is being able to identify when something just isn't working, no matter how attached you may be to it. When I was working on a series of essays for my dissertation, I spent weeks that summer tweaking a specific essay that I couldn't get right. I thought about it all the time—when I was at the supermarket or in the shower or doing the dishes—and tried to figure out what I needed to tweak to get it to feel right in my gut.

One night while we were watching TV in bed, I sat up and said, "Oh crap."

"What's wrong?" Toothpick asked as he pressed pause.

"I know what's wrong." I turned to look at him and pouted. "I have to get rid of it."

It turned out I could not be funny or unflinching or thoughtful or any of the other things I wanted to be on the page if all I was focused on was not being Myanmar. With the help of feedback from people whose opinions I valued, along with a shit ton of difficult soul-searching, I had to demonstrate to myself that I could and should have both of those things—I could have a voice that was funny and vulnerable and sharp, and that was also

Myanmar. I made my peace with this, first hesitantly, then openly, then proudly. After all, my eyes were getting tired from twitching every time another white author analyzed how enigmatic and mysterious Myanmar and our culture and people were, and I couldn't do something about it if I was so set on not writing about Myanmar (and I desperately wanted to do something about it). You hide things that you're ashamed of, and I wasn't ashamed to be Myanmar.

But my biggest fear is that it might be all or nothing— I stop being a writer altogether, or I can be a writer so long as I only write about my Brownness. I worry when I write something that doesn't have anything to do with race or, specifically, being Myanmar. I feel like I'm not working my USP. This is my marketability, this is what sets me apart on paper—and every time I write about something that doesn't draw attention to this fact with big flashing neon lights, I worry that no one will be interested in what I have to say. Every time I write something that doesn't have to do with skin-whitening creams or my grandmother's curry or interracial relationships, I'm terrified that my writing has lost its one appealing trait. And I hear it all in my head, every single possible thing that everyone else could be thinking:

Of course you sold this book—you're a great statistic.

We get it, you're Myanmar, stop pushing it in our face.

This is pretty good for a Myanmar girl.

When I shared these anxieties with T, a Myanmar American writer friend, I felt so comforted as she nodded and smiled at everything I said. A child of immigrant parents in the United States, she was the only Myanmar kid at her school in California, and so was always asked about Myanmar and Myanmar culture. She told me about how she, too, resisted incorporating Myanmarness into her writing because she felt that that was what was naturally expected of her and, to some extent, pushed upon her. The first time she and I met up, her second book was a few months away from publication, and we spent a considerable amount of our conversation gushing to each other about how excited we were for each other's books; it hit me mid-chat that this was the first time I'd ever been able to do that with another Myanmar writer. She told me that her main goal was to have power and control over her own story, and to be able to represent herself the way *she* wanted to represent herself; I marveled at her succinctness and sureness.

"I don't want this to be a race book," I told my agent Hayley at our first in-person meeting.

The story about my first encounter with Hayley is

one that I still kind of can't believe is true and that, as melodramatic as it sounds, always reaffirms my belief that the universe gives you exactly what you need, when you need it. It happened on an evening when I was still living in London, and Toothpick and I were at a screening of *The Farewell* at the ODEON on Holloway Road. In between sobbing into my popcorn (I hadn't seen A May for many months at this point), I spent the whole movie with thoughts, all along the lines of *Goddamn, this is so fucking good! I want to write a book that is this moving and charming with a full cast of Myanmar characters! Wow, wouldn't that be fucking swell, huh? Maybe one day!* When the film ended, Toothpick headed to the toilet while I waited for him in the lobby. I took out my phone to check my email, and there was a message from Hayley introducing herself and explaining that she'd read an essay of mine, one that I'd been working on for six years at that point; one that, yes, talked very much in detail about my being Myanmar.

A few weeks later, there I was in her agency's office, talking about *my* prospective *book* with her, a real agent! I kept thinking about *The Farewell*. I wanted to write a book that made people feel the things that *The Farewell* had made me feel, but I also didn't want my book to be so painfully, obviously ... Brown. I'd prepped for this meeting by going through hundreds of YouTube Q&As and blog posts and Twitter threads advising young writers on how to "sell yourself" and "play up your strengths." When I'd emailed a draft query letter to a writer friend, one of her first points of feedback was "What's going to make you stand out is that you're Myanmar, so you need to play that up more. Bring it up from the start." I knew what my USP was, and finally sitting there across from a potential agent, I didn't know if I'd just committed an act of self-sabotage by telling her that I didn't want this to be a "race book," when perhaps I should've been doing the exact opposite and playing it up.

There are days, weeks, sometimes months, where I hate everything I write. I hate the idea of representation, because if a published piece of mine sucks, will the whole world think that all Myanmar writers are bad? Sometimes I see people call for more representation across the Western artistic landscape and I hate that, too—I don't want that weight on my shoulders. When we check out of a hotel in a foreign country, Mom always makes sure to tidy up the whole room, explaining as she wipes down the bathroom counter, "If we leave this place in a mess, they'll say, 'See, *that's* what Myanmar people are like.'" When I think of my potential book in the context of representation, I want to scream to my invisible critics, "This isn't what all Myanmar women in their mid-twenties are like! If you don't believe me, ask my mother, who wonders what she, a good Buddhist who is fully committed to her family, did to

deserve such a sweary pain-in-the-ass for a daughter!"
Still, I can't shake the fear that if my book doesn't do
well, everyone else involved in the process will take it
as proof that books by Myanmar authors do not sell
(which is somewhat narcissistic of me, I concede! I'm
sorry!).

I have laughably wild fantasies about being on panels
and being interviewed on life as a writer—ideally not as
an Asian writer, a woman writer, or a Myanmar woman
writer, but just a writer. Even if I'm lucky enough to get
to that point in my life one day, I don't know whether I'll
ever be able to squash that voice in my head telling me
that I'm only ever going to be paraded out to fill the to-
ken Brown seat. People try to tell me that that's not true,
that I will succeed solely because of my talent; I don't
think I'll ever entirely believe this, because I don't think
it'll ever entirely be true—but that's something I will find
a way to make peace with, like all the writers of color I
know have done to some degree.

I have found myself being told both that I have it easy
as a writer because I am a Brown woman, *and* that I
have the odds stacked against me because I am a Brown
woman, and by the time I was working on selling my
first book, I was no longer sure whether my being Myanmar would work against, or in, my favor. I've had white
writers imply in casual conversation that I have it easy
because I have such a distinct USP. But facts state that the

opposite is true. A 2020 *New York Times* study found that in a list of English-language fiction books published between 1950 and 2018 by four of the Big Five and Doubleday, approximately 95 percent—6,767 books out of a total 7,124—were written by white authors. I read this report and cried.

When I asked myself a very basic question, "What do *you* feel when you see a Myanmar name in a bookstore?" the answer came instantly: "Surprise, and then pride." And so I had to ask myself what kind of space I would want to occupy if I had been one of the names in the 5 percent. What if I had been the *only* Myanmar name in that 5 percent? How would I make myself—not my family, not my colleagues, not even other budding Myanmar writers, but myself—proud of what I had accomplished? How would I do it: Representation without tokenization, pride without compromise?

I thought about T's words, and asked myself how, like her, I would go about gaining power and control over *my* own story. I tell people that I wish books like the ones I'm working on existed when I was a young girl, and that when I write, I write for a younger version of myself, but it turns out I was lying; I was writing for a very white audience of gatekeepers whose approval and praise I craved so that I could be deemed a *real* writer. T told me that she used to think the same way, until she realized that regardless of whether she was writing about being Myanmar to please this imaginary white audience, or not writing about it as an act of defiance, *that* specific audience and their opinions were still being centered. "I had to let go of that," she admitted. I think about that every time that I write now, and every time I wonder what an imaginary reader will think of my usage of a specific word or phrase or anecdote, I have to check in with myself and make sure that this imaginary reader looks and thinks a lot like a thirteen-year-old version of me, and not some generic old white dude.

When I was younger, Mom and I visited Singapore every year to see my uncle and his family. My favorite part of these summer breaks was the bookstores. I'd spend the weeks leading up to our next trip writing down a list of books that I wanted to buy on a lined sheet of A4 that I then folded up into a small square and tucked into my small crossbody bag. I always bugged Mom to let me hit up all the highlights: Popular, Kinokuniya, Borders (RIP), even the small music memoir section of HMV. It took me until my teens to dream of maybe, possibly, just perhaps, having my own name printed on an actual book in a real-life bookstore. A book not in the Country Guides or Geography or Politics section where, of course, you'd expect to find a book about Myanmar, but in the general Fiction or Nonfiction section, where there didn't *need* to be a book by a Myanmar writer, especially not someone youngish, someone who was pretty average and wasn't writing about how they led a rebellion or were a descendant of the Burmese royal family. Another thing T told me has also stuck with me (she's very wise), and I repeat it to myself like a mantra: "I wanted to be visible to people who needed to see me, not people who didn't *want* to see me."

I can be competitive, to the point where sometimes I lose sight of what's important. I've never admitted this to anyone because I'm aware of what a terrible person this makes me sound like, but the whole time I was working on this book, there was an ugly knot in my stomach that was a result of the worry that another Myanmar writer, especially if they were another young, female Myanmar writer, would put their work out on submission at the same time as me. The chances that a publisher would want to publish two "Myanmar books" (or, perhaps even two "Southeast Asian books") in one year were devastatingly slim, I knew from studying the trends and speaking with non-white writer friends. This was, after all, my *unique* selling point. Am I allowed to say that? Does that break some sort of code of solidarity among writers of color? That is a hypothetical question, because I know it does, and I am working every day to dissect and deprogram this repugnant part of my brain. I want to publish many books, and it is terrifying and heartbreaking, and also infuriating, to think that I might be turned down solely because another Myanmar writer *beat me to it*. Of course, I'd also be happy that one of *ours* had gotten a deal—another Myanmar name to run my fingers along in a bookstore. But it makes me ashamed (and rightfully so, and I will never stop chastising myself for this) to admit that hypothetical me feels a lot less happy than she should be, and that that burst of pride is tainted by a grotesque shade of envy. I have to remind myself that competitiveness is good, but not when you are competing with the wrong people, or when you are participating in a competition that you should be working to dismantle altogether.

I have to remind myself that *I* shouldn't be one of the voices that frames my ethnicity as my unique selling point, or at least, as my *only* selling point, and that the weight of representation will be much easier to bear if and when I can share it with others. MiMi told me that it took her agent years to sell *Mandalay* because they'd kept being told that, although her writing was beautiful, Myanmar food (and thus a Myanmar cookbook) was "too niche" or that "nobody's heard of Myanmar," that there was "no market" for it. Then, after all those years, Myanmar food started becoming trendy in England— there were a couple of hip new restaurants, a few pop-ups, white chefs and food writers were mentioning the cuisine in national papers—and so MiMi was finally offered a book deal, being the recognized authority in the United Kingdom. When *Mandalay* came out, it was the first Myanmar cookbook to be published by a U.K. publisher *ever*; the only other one had been a self-published book that had come out about a decade earlier.

By the time I sold my first book and thought about working on a second, the first decision I made was that it would be a commercial fictional work set in Myanmar. When I emailed over the first few chapters of my novel to my best friends, the first thing that one of them texted me was "Are you going to keep the Myanmar names?"

I replied: "Yes. Because they are Myanmar lol."

She immediately texted back: "Good."

Iow many cups of rice do I eat?" I ask Mom as I scroll through the different rice cookers being sold on Amazon. "For a meal? Every day? I don't know. Two cups?" she guesses. My mother can answer 99 percent of the questions that I throw at her—*How do I repaint a wall? What kind of toothpaste do I buy? How do I say "food poisoning" in French?*—but this fell within the 1 percent. At home, A May measures rice not in cups, but in noe si buus. (Who needs to buy specifically marked measuring cups when you can just reuse an empty condensed milk can? Myanmar ingenuity at its finest!) Two noe si buus are usually enough to feed the entire family for the day, but she'll put on three if we're expecting guests.

After all, Myanmar people don't eat cups of rice, we eat plates of rice—large, round, white porcelain plates with small blue flowers that were handed down to our grandparents by their parents and that have slightly chipped raised rims so that all of that rice doesn't spill over. We love rice so much that someone took the time to come up with two different names for it: cooked rice is htamin, and raw rice grains are san.

Rice keeps both our homes and our country running—we export several million tons of rice every year, and in 2017, we were the seventh-highest rice-producing country in the world. Whether you're seeing the country through the window of a plane or car or train, you will always see the sun rise and set behind acres of green paddy fields. Our ancestors have planted and harvested and cooked rice for centuries. Today, even an American born and bred brand such as KFC cannot ignore Myanmar's love of rice, adapting their local menu to include options like a Rice Box with Potato Curry and Chicken Popcorn, and a simple six-hundred-kyat bowl of rice filed under Sides & Snacks. Our Myanmar tongues and taste buds are fluent in rice; we learned it before we learned the alphabet. We love it so much that it's seeped into our language; when we ask someone if they've already eaten, we say "Htamin sar bi pyi lar?"—literally "Have you eaten rice?" It's unthinkable that you would have a meal that wasn't primarily made up of, or at the very least included, rice. In fact, mealtime in general is called htamin sar chain: "time to eat rice."

Whenever there is any kind of nationwide disruption—political unrest, or a natural disaster, for example—the first thing A May yells is, "How much rice do we have?" and she sends us to the shops to buy five times the amount that we think we'll need. In their personal account for *The New York Times* of the first day of the 2021 coup, journalist Aye Min Thant recalled what every household in the country was muttering as they scrambled to the market that morning: "You can survive a curfew, a long crackdown, if you have enough rice." A family friend didn't find out about the coup until around noon, at which point every store in his neighborhood was out of rice and he had to go to another part of the city to purchase it. "San, see, sar—if you have that, you can survive anything," A May always says; rice, of course, and salt and oil because you need *some* form of seasoning.

I did not know how much I loved rice until I moved to countries where rice was only really had when you got Chinese takeout. A May is old-fashioned and refuses to use a rice cooker ("It sucks out all of the nutrients!" she claims, huffing and puffing when I ask her to *please* explain the scientific logic behind her statement), but when I found myself with neither the time nor the energy to make rice her way every day, I half-heartedly purchased my very first rice cooker. The first time I used the three-hundred-millileter-capacity contraption, I pored over the accompanying instruction sheet for an embarrassingly long period of time; I'm good with technology and can set up most consoles without consulting the manual, but I had no clue how to operate this tiny plastic white pot in front of me. It had two clips on each side that held down the lid, which had four little slots on top to let the steam escape. It was made up of twelve parts, each one drawn and labeled in black and white on the guide, along with step-by-step instructions that referred to the corresponding numbered parts:

1. Measure your rice using the Measuring Cup.[11] Rinse the rice in cold water and place into the Inner Pot.[3] Add water.
2. Plug in the Power Cable[12] and connect to the power socket. The "Warm" Light[8] will illuminate.
3. Press the Cook Button[6] down. The "Cook" Light[7] will illuminate and the cooking process will start.
4. When the rice is cooked, the Cook Button[6] will move back to the ready position and the "Cook" Light[7] will switch off. The "Warm" Light[8] will illuminate, showing that the cooker is keeping the rice warm.

In addition to the dreaded cups, there were lids and pots and lights and a whole lot of jargon that I had never previously contended with when making rice. Nonetheless, once I mastered how to operate it, and as Mom predicted when she bought me the device, I ended up using my rice cooker almost every day, making sure not to get the burnt bottom layer when I scraped my freshly cooked htamin into my large but rimless turquoise IKEA plate for almost every meal.

Toothpick jokes that if I get to choose where we're going out to eat, it's "always Thai or Chinese," to which I roll my eyes and reply, "Yes, because they have the best rice." My favorite neighborhood in London is Chinatown (how Asian of me), and when he and I eat at a restaurant there and he orders his usual three-combination barbecued meat and says "That's it" to the server, I can't help but prompt, "You don't want any rice?"; I know he hasn't forgotten, but still, I feel the need to ask *just in case.*

In my opinion, rice is practically perfect no matter what form it takes. Congee is soothing when you're ill or just cold and want something with more oomph than soup. You can taste all the different herbs and spices that go into a plate of biryani in just that first bite. The layer of crispy, crackling rice is a wonderful treat when you get to the bottom of your bowl of bibimbap. Rice pudding is the perfect combination of sweet and savory in one dessert. Mom and I enjoy snacking on dried rice cakes on long flights.

To be Myanmar means to love rice. To be a Myanmar woman, specifically, and insofar as I've observed in our home, means to know how to make rice and to ensure that there is always a pot of rice on standby; it also means to know that you are not allowed to help yourself to this rice that you've just steamed to perfection, or at least, not as freely as you would maybe like.

I love how on a universal level, everyone agrees that it's funny when kids—and I mean *actual* kids, not teenagers—swear. When a three-year-old girl won't stop saying "Fuck!" or "You bitch!" in public, all the adults laugh. It's funny because she doesn't know better, doesn't know that people, especially little girls, shouldn't say those words, and especially in front of others. In a decade's time, it will no longer be funny, and will instead be inappropriate and rude and unbecoming of a young woman. But for now, it's hilarious.

I can't remember a time when I wasn't aware of the fact that my body is approximately thirty pounds heavier than it *should* be. I've always loved eating A May's rice and curries, but the older I got, the more conscious I became of how much space my body took up, and the more ashamed I felt about how much I loved food. I used to wonder if things would have turned out differently for me if I hadn't been raised by a grandma who took immense pride in keeping me well fed. Mom says that when I was a kid and before I knew how to speak, I would point to my mouth to indicate that I was hungry, and A May would rectify the situation by feeding me her htamin with fish curry. So how bizarre it was when I became an adult who *could* speak, and found myself increasingly hesitant to say the words "Htamin sar chin tae." It was as though I was a toddler again, one who was unable to utter something as simple as "I'm hungry" or "I want to eat," only now it was because whenever I expressed that I was hungry, people would jokingly reply, "You're always hungry." The script was always the same. "Htamin sar chin tae," I'd say as I got home from school and peered into the various pots and skillets in which A May had been cooking all day, and Mom would roll her eyes and remark that I always wanted to eat. Everyone seemed to be in on this collective joke, and I began to think that it was probably true. It seemed like such a shame that I had to control myself when we had so much rice at the ready, but I was told that it was much more shameful to be a fat girl who devours rice.

There is a very specific look that a Myanmar auntie's face can't help but give away when a woman, especially a young girl who's already fat, who was born fat, tells her, "I like food. I want to eat food." Htamin sar chin tae. The look is a bit of shock and disgust, but it's mainly pity: *This poor fat girl will never find a good husband, or even a boyfriend. If only she could control herself and eat less rice.* It's the look that they get when they realize that the potty-mouthed three-year-old girl has turned into a sweary thirteen-year-old who still doesn't know better. Better fix that, and fast. And so they did, or at least they tried to. "Eat less rice." "Eat only brown rice."

"Don't eat rice at night." "Eat your rice slooooowly so that your stomach will think it's full." I was advised to eat less food in general, but was given specific instructions to stay away from the rice. When I tried to eat less curry or skip dessert instead, I was reminded that it was the rice that was making me fat. Believe it or not, the joy of catching up with extended family members whom you only see a few times a year is swiftly diminished when the rice crock comes around the table, and the first thing they tell you before you've even finished scooping up a spoon is "You should eat less rice" or "Wow, that's a lot of rice." Oftentimes, I want to stab the table with my fork and yell, "I thought this was supposed to be a *meal* where people *eat*, so can you please just let me eat my fucking rice in fucking peace?"

But I knew I couldn't give up the rice, so instead I tried a lot of other tricks to make up for my failure. My daily go-to for several years was sucking in my stomach whenever I went out; it became second nature, and I didn't even realize how well I had trained my body to do it as soon as I stepped foot outside the house, until I could no longer remember the last time that I crawled into bed at night without aching from moderate to severe cramps. As a proud night owl, I would be grateful to my body for sleeping until 10:00 or 11:00 a.m., thereby prompting me to only have to eat two meals a day. I wore jeans that I knew were one to two sizes too small and that I had to take a deep breath and suck in my fat stomach to button up, but what's a pair of skinny jeans without some skin pinching? It's in the name, after all—*skinny* jeans.

Khin and I have been best friends since we were five years old, and like I've always been fat, she's always been skinny; when we were children, the contrast between our bodies was "funny" given how close we were. When we got older, it became less and less funny every time someone pointed it out. I was never jealous of Khin for being skinny—she had her own share of unwanted comments regarding her body to deal with because being a woman is always a joy—but I *was* jealous of her fast metabolism, and how she could eat and eat and still her stomach remained flat and the gap between her thighs never disappeared. "How are you so skinny when you eat so much?" people would marvel at her. Or they'd say, "Wow, you're so lucky that you can eat so much and still be so skinny!"—I noticed that older aunties, in particular, would say this with a tinge of envy. I knew it wasn't her fault that she was naturally skinny but my first reflex whenever she stated that she was hungry was to get angry, because whenever *she* got hungry, *she* got to eat. My anger should've been directed at the fatphobic and misogynistic society that made me think eating when you're hungry is wrong, but at fourteen, it's hard to not be angry when it seems like you and your best friend have to follow different guidelines regarding hunger. After all, did you know that it's impolite—sometimes even inappropriate—for a woman to say that she's hungry?

Younger me used to love tagging along to lunches or dinners with Mom and her girlfriends; it made me feel like an adult as I soaked up all of the *adult* gossip that was being exchanged at these *adult* gatherings. The downside of these meals, though, was that I also had to watch them—these strong, successful grown-ups—carve out a portion of their agenda to lightly scold themselves for eating, and make a near-performance out of saying, "Oh no, I shouldn't be eating so much rice, look how fat I've gotten lately," at which point others would chime in and say, "Me too," and suddenly, at least for a few minutes, it turned into a competition of who could berate themselves the most. I'd always think I was doing something wrong for *not* feeling like that as I continued eating. After a while, the gossip, as salacious as it could be, just wasn't worth it anymore. As I distanced myself from conversations like these in any social situation, but especially ones that involved meals, I started to wonder to what extent debates around hunger and food come up when men sit down for a meal. I noticed a dark dilemma that many mothers faced as their daughters got older: a conflict between wanting to teach their daughter to be a beautiful and proper woman who doesn't openly admit their love of eating, particularly in social circles, and the maternal instinct to keep your child well fed.

I have observed mothers beam when people tell them that their daughter is so pretty, which is followed by the elucidation that she is so skinny, almost like a pat on the back for both mother and daughter; I used to wonder— and if I'm being honest, maybe I still do in the back of my mind every once in a while—if Mom ever wished that people would say that about me. Everyone says that food connects people, but sometimes it estranges us too.

When I first moved abroad and people asked me what I missed most about home, it was a no-brainer: "The food." I'd chuckle to myself when I gave that answer, because when I was a child, I was obsessed with spaghetti and hot dogs and burgers (there was one single burger joint in town, called Burger Busters, that Mom would sometimes take us to after school as a special treat) and all the other white people food that I'd see American kids eating in the movies. I thought that when I finally moved abroad as an adult, I would stuff myself full of all of these delicious doughy carbs and survive exclusively on McDonald's and Subway. And for the first few months, that's exactly what I did; on our first date, my then-boyfriend took me to Subway (we were on a student budget!), and it made me smile because this was exactly the kind of thing that, again, I'd seen white teenagers do in the movies. But then, after those couple of months, I found myself physically craving rice. When my boyfriend asked where I wanted to go for dinner, I'd suggest Siam

Square in the Great Barrington town center, or The East across from (get this) the McDonald's. Eating rice in this white town where I was almost always surrounded by white people (bar the Asian staff at these restaurants) was a new experience, and one that was . . . nice. While I asked for a second order of rice, no one was judging me, or making passive-aggressive comments, or flat-out telling me I should stop. You know how if you're going through a rough patch in a relationship, sometimes the best thing to do is take some time apart and figure yourselves out separately before getting back together? Yeah, *that*. It took my leaving Myanmar and spending the next several years living in countries where I had to plan at least half an hour ahead if I wanted to have rice, for me to realize how much I had taken for granted a home where there was always a giant pot of it, not to mention a country where people just ask you several times a day in passing, "Have you eaten rice?" Absence and a fonder heart, right? When you are left entirely to your own devices in the middle of a giant Tesco or Price Chopper, it's interesting to see which aisles your brain and body head for. Living by myself, my go-to meals were fried rice with chili oil and a sunny-side up egg on top, or steamed rice with a packet of Indomie Mi Goreng. I am not a foodie or even a remotely adept chef, and I turned to rice because yes, it is comforting and something that my tongue knows and craves, but also because it is easy and most importantly, filling. I was reminded that *that* is why rice is aplenty in Myanmar—because it is good at filling you and quieting the rumbles in your stomach, the way food and the act of nourishing yourself should.

Toothpick is a picky eater (not as picky as he was when I first found him, thank god, but still), and nine times out of ten, will default to the nearest McDonald's if it were left entirely up to him to choose our next meal—for him, a Big Mac is the safest bet; I used to berate him for this, but I've noticed over the years that no matter what city *I'm* in, *my* brain registers a Chinese or Thai or, really, any Asian restaurant as the safe choice—my criterion for safe means I know they will have rice, because let's be honest, it would require a great deal of incompetence on a chef's part to fuck up a plate of fried rice. I smile when I sit down at one of these establishments and see the table setting: a plate in the middle, a fork to the left, and a spoon to the right; there's also probably a knife, but I know I won't use it. I had gotten caught up in all of the different voices telling me to love rice because this is my heritage, or to always keep it at arm's length, or to have some but not *too much*, or to know how to make it because I am a woman but not have it myself, or—; I needed to remove myself from the noise to be able to hear my own thoughts, and once I did, it was clear: htamin sar chin tae.

I have spent the last several years trying to be kinder to myself, to treat myself at the dinner table the way, well, the way men and "growing boys" are treated. We never debate men's hunger; wives serve up rice to their husbands and take pride when their partners gobble down their hard work. Whenever I'm in the middle of a meal and someone tells me that I should ease up on the rice, the stubborn, petty part of me makes a point to eat that little bit more. I no longer try to contain my audible squeals when I see that A May has cooked my favorite dishes. When another auntie in the room says with a small, self-conscious chuckle, "I'm hungry, but I shouldn't eat this," I shake my head and reply, "You should. If you're hungry, you should eat." Some of them shake their head back and laugh like you do when a child says "Shiiiit!" without knowing what *shit* even means. But some look at me and smile and reply with a small, startled laugh, "You have a point," and put that spoon of htamin in their mouth. When I moved back to Yangon, I had changed in so many ways, one of them being that I kept my promise to myself to never take a pot brimming with rice for granted ever again. I still see the fear—fear of tiny rice grains, can you imagine?—on people's faces on a near-daily basis though, and each time, I am right back at the table with my mother and her friends: grown women telling other women to eat less rice, to not eat at night, to stop eating before you're full, to eat slowly and drink more water to trick your brain into thinking it's full; I can't decide if it makes me angrier when they do this to young women or to other grown adult women. Women are consistently accused of being *hangry*, but of course we get hangry. Look what you've turned us into.

When I moved back to Yangon, I decided that, in an effort to push myself to be more independent, I'd limit the number of meals I had at my parents'. By now, I had moved into my own place, and A May's main concern— second to a home invasion in the middle of the night— was that I would starve to death. When my parents told friends that I'd moved out, they would ask, "How does she cook?" and then joke, "Oh well, maybe she'll lose some weight," the punchline being that I didn't know how to cook. Joke's on them—I lost no weight because A May took it as a personal insult whenever I called in the morning to say I wasn't coming over for food. These days, she rings me, her twenty-something adult grand-daughter, at lunchtime and again at dinnertime and tells me that she's going to send over some food to my place; she is also very sneaky and only calls me once she's al-ready cooked the food so that I feel too guilty to say no.

"No," I try. "I've already eaten."

"What did you eat?"

"Pizza."

She tuts and asks how that's going to be filling—to her, rice is the only filling carbohydrate in the world. She says she will send over a potato curry and an egg curry and some htamin. She can't control what time I come home or if my room is warm enough or if I'm ironing my clothes, but she can at least make sure I'm fed. If a man breaks into my home in the middle of the night and kills me in my sleep, at least I'll die with a full stomach.

Whenever I returned home from college for a school break, or even now, when I come back from a holiday, A May is the first person I run to. She's not particularly into physical love languages, but when I throw my arms around her large waist, my hands barely touching each other, and bury my head between her head and her shoulder, she plants a kiss on my cheek. I grab her hands, which are always rough and dry from being washed multiple times a day before touching the food, and rub her arms that are covered in scars from hot oil splashes, all of which she wears like badges of honor tattooed onto her skin. Sometimes she tries to back away, insisting, "A May chway dway kyi bae," but I don't care that she's drenched in sweat and that each pore in her body seems to be emanating the scent of one of a million different curries. And regardless of how long it's been since I've showered or whether it's 1:00 p.m. or 1:00 a.m., the first question she asks is "Htamin sar ma lar?"

"Hote, htamin sar chin tae," I reply with a grin, as I realize it's been days or weeks or sometimes *months* since someone asked me if I want to eat htamin. Of course I want to eat rice. I want to eat *your* rice. I always want to eat your rice.

TONGUE TWISTERS

When he was a kid, Phyo couldn't say the letter င in the Myanmar alphabet. It sounds similar to another letter, ည, but they are two different letters, like *D* and *T*. Native English speakers who take Myanmar language lessons always struggle with င because the sound doesn't exist in the English language; their tongue simply doesn't know how to position itself to make that particular noise. For some reason, Phyo was the only one out of the three of us whose tongue was physically incapable of pronouncing this one letter. At lunch and dinner, we would tease him and tell him to say င, and every time he would say ည, and we would laugh and do it again.

"င."

"ည."

"င."

"ည." As we laughed, my brother kept going, again and again, mainly to himself now. ည. ည. ည. Nyaaar.

No, we would say. When you say ည, your tongue starts out at the roof of your mouth. When you say င, your tongue is suspended midair and requires the most minuscule of movements. My brother would think about it as he said it over and over again, until it no longer sounded like an actual letter and simply became a random sound that he was trying to imitate. It frustrated him. All our tongues knew how to make this sound, but his didn't.

Toothpick introduces me to people as Pyae with a hard *P*, and I never correct him. I don't comment that if you say Pyae with a hard *P*, then you're actually saying a different word in Myanmar, you're saying "slow." A hard *P* requires you to start with your lips firmly pressed against each other. In Myanmar, a hard *P* and a soft *P* are two separate letters of the alphabet: ပ and ဖ. It's subtle but important, and every Myanmar person knows the difference between the two.

I can't recall if, on the first day of my first undergraduate class (in that then-still-terrifyingly-new-to-me country), when we had to go around and do the customary self-introductions, I introduced myself with two hard *P*s or two soft *P*s. After all, it was difficult enough to get people to say and remember how to pronounce "Pyae," and insisting that they do it with a soft *P* as well seemed like an insignificant battle to be picking. Four years later though, on the first day of my MA course in London, I said, "Hi, I'm Pyae Pyae." Pyae Pyae with two hard *P*s. I didn't even stop to think about it. It used to be that I was Pyae with a hard *P* if a friend from abroad was saying my name, and Pyae with a soft *P* when I was saying it myself, but somehow, I too began self-censoring and saying "slow" instead of "full." It's worked its way into my speech, or at least when I'm speaking English with non-Myanmar people. My brain makes the switch without thinking twice.

Actress Ania Marson once said that a noticeable physical shift is involved when you take on an accent for a role, and that your entire mouth alters itself in order to accommodate this new, different accent; if you are doing the accent properly, you almost transform into a different person, and, I assume, get one step closer to *becoming* the character you're playing. I wonder what kind of minuscule physical shifts that I've never noticed take place when I talk to someone who knows me as Pyae Pyae with two hard *P*s. I wonder how different hard-*P* Pyae and soft-*P* Pyae really are.

Once, Khin and I met up with a friend of hers for a book event in London, and when we took our seats, Khin said, "This is Pyae" with a soft *P*. Her friend wasn't Myanmar, she probably couldn't make or distinguish the soft *P* sound, but it didn't matter to Khin; to her, I was Pyae, specifically, soft-*P* Pyae. I was so accustomed to introducing myself or being introduced as Pyae with a hard *P* to anyone who wasn't Myanmar that I actually paused for a couple of seconds. *Oh,* I remember thinking. *Right. That's what it's supposed to sound like.*

In the Myanmar language, there is no such sound as an *R*, let alone *rrr.* A Myanmar person would pronounce *super* as "supah." It's why I've always thought it weird when some Myanmar people refer to the city as Rangoon when they're writing or speaking in English. When I spell Moe Thet War in Myanmar, it's pronounced "Moe Thet Wah." When native English speakers say my name, to my ears it always sounds like they're emphasizing that last *R*. In class, at the doctor's, at the nail salon—"Miss War? Is there a Miss War here?" Miss War. War. Warr. Miss Phyae Phyae Warr. The way their tongue curls around that last letter makes me wince.

I like to joke that whenever I visit Toothpick's Very White hometown, I raise their Asian population to double digits. When I go into a shop, I'm usually one of two or three—or a lot of times, the only—non-white people in the whole place. Most of the staff and customers glance or stare as I make my way down an aisle. When I go to the cash register to pay, I give my perfected warm smile and say in my American accent, "Hiya, just this, please." I watch them relax. At least I am an educated, *good* Asian who speaks *proper* English that they can understand. At least I'm an Asian *American* well versed in Western culture, and not an Asian *Asian,* complete with an Asian accent. And I relax, too, when I see that they are relaxed, that they are treating me with courtesy.

One study showed that to non-Americans, American accents are most likely to be perceived as friendly, straightforward, and assertive. A Spanish accent is considered the *most* friendly, a German accent is the *most* straightforward and professional, a Swedish accent is trustworthy, and French and Italian accents are the most stylish. All this to say—certain cultural markers instantly earn you respect and access, while others do the opposite. After all, I have Australian and French friends who moved abroad and retained their accents, but their accents were always hailed as sophisticated and cool, while any trace of a Myanmar accent would be viewed as backward or uneducated. When Toothpick and I first started dating, my non-British friends would always point to his accent as a plus, reiterating that near-worldwide perception that British accents are sexy; no one's ever described a Myanmar accent as sexy, or if they have, I certainly haven't come across such an account.

When I get in a taxi in England or the United States or any predominantly Caucasian country, the first thing I say is a loud and crisp "Hello!" and then I enunciate exactly where I want to go, projecting my voice a tiny bit more than I do in everyday conversation. All of a sudden, I am friendly, I am straightforward, I am assertive. I am not usually a loud or slow speaker, nor a fan of small talk, but if I have to talk loudly and clearly (but still in a casual manner like I'm from *around here*) about the weather or traffic for a few minutes so that I'm not stuck at the receiving end of some xenophobic remark once I've paid the fare, then sign me up. (The best-case scenario is that this is all in my head and people aren't as racist as I always fear, but better to err on the side of caution.) When we visit Toothpick's parents and get into a taxi at the train station, I always stay silent and let *him* tell the driver where we're going. He has never asked me why I don't just give the address myself, especially if I'm the first between the two of us to get in the car. I don't know if he's ever noticed. But I do, because it is a very precise, conscious decision. I also notice that, in the middle of the ride, I make a point to talk to him about something small that happened on our journey or ask what our dinner plans that evening will be, so that this complete stranger in the driver's seat knows that I can speak English well, that I can speak it without an accent, so that I can let them assume that I'm American and consequently put them at ease with my supposed proximity to whiteness.

Toothpick's family will tell you about the time we had dinner at a small family-run Indian restaurant down the road from their house. After giving our food orders, I said that for a drink, I'd be fine with just some "war-ter." Toothpick pronounces *water* without the *T*; they all do (apparently in England, it's a distinct regional accent marker). "Wah-er." And when I said I wanted some "war-ter," it was as though I had taken off some mask that I'd been unknowingly wearing all evening, and had at last revealed my true self, which was someone who was not from around here as evidenced by how I say *water.*

"I'm sorry?" The waitress paused and smiled. "What was it you wanted?"

"Um, the water?" I repeated.

She laughed. Not a mean or mocking laugh, just a laugh. "I love it! Say it again?" "War-ter," I repeated with a smile and now the whole table laughed. When she ran into Toothpick's mom on the street several months later, she said, "Oh I know you! How's the girl who wanted the *war-ter*?"

Toothpick's family teases me about my accent a lot, which is honestly fine. No one says anything mean, and I like to mock them as well when I ask for a cup of "wah-er." But to this day, I find myself thinking about that waitress and her response to my accent. Like me, she was Brown, specifically Indian, with a British accent. I wonder if she makes an intentional effort to put white customers at ease with her accent, if that's why her parents put her in charge of waiting on tables.

The Chinese place down the other end of the road from Toothpick's parents' house has some of the best Chinese food I've ever had in my life. They've been operating a long time, I'm told. The owners and chefs are all of Chinese descent, but a young white woman with an English accent answers the phone and greets customers. They only do takeout, so their phone is always busy.

"I don't mean to be racist—" one of Toothpick's relatives once began as we were getting ready to call up the restaurant (this was before they'd hired a white woman to answer the phones); I immediately braced myself for something racist, as all people of color instinctually do when you hear those six words. They finished the sentence with, "But I really struggle to understand what they say on the phone." Toothpick replied, "No, actually, that's kind of racist," but I just gave a polite smile; I still scold myself for that. Sometimes we'd go over and place an order in person, and I'd make a point to smile at the Chinese woman behind the counter and nod breezily as she recited my order back to me; of course she had an accent, but so did every other white person in town, and if I'm expected to concentrate to understand what the girl with the Irish accent at McDonald's is saying to me, then I have to do the same here, too.

I wonder when that restaurant realized that they needed to have someone with a British accent taking the orders. Had there been customers who had had the audacity to voice a complaint? Or had every Chinese employee who'd been assigned phone duty gotten tired of having to repeat themselves multiple times to the increasingly agitated white person on the other end of the line? It doesn't matter that they make the best chicken fried rice in town. No one wants to order takeout from the restaurant that they can't understand. In 1981, Manuel Fragante, a Filipino immigrant in the United States, applied for a job at the Department of Motor Vehicles. He scored the highest on a written civil service test that was taken by over seven hundred other applicants, but was turned down after the hiring managers brought him in for an interview. Fragante filed a lawsuit, and in court, it was revealed that during his interview, the interviewers wrote down "difficult manner of pronunciation" and "heavy Filipino [accent]." During the trial, professional linguists testified that, grammatically, Fragante's English was perfect. However, the defendants argued that "the DMV is a place of high-stress, short-term interactions with an often unreasonable public. Communication is the essence of the job." And you cannot communicate if you speak English with an accent, despite the fact that throughout the entire trial, no one—from the court reporter to the judge to the lawyers present—had any trouble understanding Fragante's speech.

On Toothpick's first trip to Yangon, I'd have to keep switching between a conversation with him and another one with A May. There were a lot of things she wanted to know about him.

"Ask him," I told her one afternoon. She isn't fully fluent in English, but she can maintain a basic conversation. She smiled. I pressed, "No, ask him, it's fine."

"He won't understand me," she told me in Myanmar.

"Of course he will!" I said quickly, perhaps too quickly, perhaps to cover up the fact that few things in the world made me sadder than my grandmother thinking that her accent wasn't clear enough or proper enough or up to par for anyone, let alone a twenty-something white British dude, boyfriend or not. A May taught me English before I even went to school, and now, in retrospect, I question if she refrained from speaking too much English in front of me in case I started to pick up her accented English.

So, she asked Toothpick a question, and he responded, "Sorry, what was that?" She smiled and repeated herself, and he paused for a few seconds to try to understand before answering. I know he wasn't aware of the context of everything that was happening, but I wanted to stab him in the eye with my fork.

I was still thinking about it later that evening when we were hanging out at my place. I knew I needed to bring it up; mispronouncing my name because you are physically incapable of doing otherwise is one thing, but this is the kind of nonsense that leads to you becoming an adult man who thinks that you can say something racist about a person's accent and brush it off with "I don't mean to be racist, but—."

"You should make more of an effort to understand people's accents," I said. I didn't know how to say it nicely or without making him uncomfortable. I didn't know how to say it without making him feel shitty, but sometimes even the people you love need to feel shitty about doing shitty things.

"What do you mean?" he asked.

"I mean like earlier, when my grandmother had to repeat herself every time she asked you something. You do it a lot." He does do it a lot. "I don't like it."

"I'm sorry. I don't mean to do it on purpose."

I nodded. "I know. But you need to try harder."

I've encountered enough racist microaggressions to no longer believe that a lack of malicious intentions serves as a blanket excuse. It's been proven that due to an "accent gap" in their programming, smart speakers like Amazon's Alexa and the Google Home have the most trouble understanding Chinese and Spanish accents (despite the fact that, at least as of 2019, those are the two most common first languages in the world). Then again, it's no secret that Silicon Valley is still overwhelmingly white, so is it really a surprise that tech created by upper-middle-class white people in California and Washington also primarily caters to people who speak like upper-middle-class white people from California and Washington?

A friend's dad routinely rants about how his car's GPS

system is racist and doesn't understand his Indian accent. In a *Washington Post* article on accents and smart speakers, one person admitted: "When you're in a social situation, you're more reticent to use [the speaker] because you think, 'This thing isn't going to understand me and people are going to make fun of me, or they'll think I don't speak that well.'" Sure, theoretically speaking, the real message here should be *Shame on these tech bros for not being able to create a "smart" speaker that understands more than one vaguely defined group of accents!* But of course, the tech bros of Silicon Valley don't care, and the embarrassment is most felt by the users who move their lips and tongues in slightly different manners from them. Several of my writer friends, who are also not white and fully fluent in English, find that in a social setting abroad, as soon as they speak with their non-American, non-Western accent (my, say, French friends don't seem to ever encounter this dilemma), people switch off. It's wrong and infuriating, but my friends just roll their eyes and say that it's okay, they're used to it. This is why they stick to writing. If some of the most advanced technology we have today isn't wired to understand non-native accents, think of what that says about human brains. In the mid-to-late 1980s, there was, as the *Los Angeles Times* described it, a "growing national outcry" from North American students over the accents of foreign graduate students who were also working as teaching assistants.

There were so many complaints that in 1986, a group of Illinois lawmakers proposed a vague law that required state-run colleges to guarantee that all of their teaching staff were proficient in oral English without actually clarifying the level of proficiency someone was supposed to meet. One senator who voted in favor of the bill claimed that their students "shouldn't have to be guinea pigs for foreigners trying to learn English." Another who opposed it pleaded:

> Many of us on this floor are first-generation Americans. Our parents spoke with accents. Our grandparents spoke with accents. These people will be precluded from teaching in an institution of higher education, if this motion prevails. You might be able to teach someone grammar, you might be able to teach them punctuation and spelling, but you can't remove an accent from an adult after they have learned English following learning a foreign language or another language as a child ... Unfortunately, this legislation is very well-meaning, but unfortunately, it is not going to remedy the problem, and it will be discriminatory against people whose only crime is that they speak with an accent.

The bill passed. What was most interesting to me about the *Times* article, though, was that it also pointed out that of the dozen-plus students they'd interviewed who had complained about "Asian" teachers who spoke with accents, not one person could tell them the specific nationality of the instructor they were criticizing.

Following this nationwide outcry, one particular study looked at the role that "nonlanguage factors" play in others' judgments of a person's intelligibility. A group of sixty-two students was divided into two smaller groups, and each group listened to one of two prerecorded short lectures that had been made by the same native English speaker who had been raised in Ohio and was a doctoral student in speech communication. At the same time, each group was shown a picture of the lecturer they were listening to—Group A saw a photo of a Caucasian woman, and Group B, a Chinese woman. After their respective lectures, both groups had to take a short exam. Group B's marks were significantly lower than Group A's. Group B, believing they were listening to a non-Caucasian speaker, had noted "accent differences" that did not actually exist, and as a result, "their listening comprehension appeared to be undermined simply by identifying (visually) the instructor as Asian." In other words, they saw an Asian woman, assumed she spoke English with an "Asian" accent, and their brain accordingly responded as though it were receiving information through an accent that it decided it could not fully understand without even trying to listen in the first place. Why make the effort if you already *know* from first glance that someone is going to be speaking "with an accent"?

But we can never win, right? Priyanka Chopra admitted that when she first started out in Hollywood, casting directors would ask her to "use your Indian accent," to which she would reply, "I *am* speaking in my Indian accent. This is how we speak in modern India!" And then, when she was announced for the lead role in *Quantico*, Indian media were quick to point out her clear-cut American accent, forcing her to admit in another interview that her character did require "an American accent, a little bit more than my natural one!" Imagine what a constant, exhausting tightrope we're always having to tread as we figure out which accent will serve us best in which situations.

Speaking from experience, if I had to make a list of the top five things about myself that have served me the most throughout my life, my American accent could very easily rank number one. It used to be something I was so proud of too. Before I learned about microaggressions, I believed that "You have an American accent!" or "How come you don't speak with an accent?" were legitimate compliments. It made my parents and grandmother proud as well. As a kid, they would push me to say something in English in front of their friends, and beam at my flawless American English. I did my undergrad in a small, very white town in the Berkshires of western Massachusetts. On one of my first days, a staff member with whom I was having a very brief introductory conversation said as a compliment, "I would've believed you if you said you were from Vermont!" I fit right in.

When I was close to finishing my graduate program in London and began remotely applying for jobs back in Yangon, I have no doubt that my accent helped me secure a well-paid job without the hiring manager even needing to meet me in person. In our Skype interview, I answered all of their questions with my American-accented English. The role was a marketing position at a company with an open-floor office plan. The place was filled with three long tables around which everyone worked; the marketing team took up half of a table, while the other two and a half were occupied by the sales team. I chose writing as a career because I'm not a massive fan of talking to people, which was why I was also consistently in awe of every salesperson in that office who was almost always on the phone. Most of my work was online, but there were times when I would have to call someone or, as was more the case, my white boss would come over to discuss something with me.

About a month after I'd started working there, and once I became comfortable with my colleagues, I was having a casual chat with someone from the sales team when he said something along the lines of "We're always talking about how you speak so quickly. It's so cool. You sound just like an American." I thanked him, but my cheeks were burning. I listened to them on their calls, but I didn't think they were all listening to me, too. I didn't think they all noticed.

Despite the accent coming in handy, it bothers me when people think I'm American. I want to follow up and tell them that no, I'm not American, I'm just able to adopt the accent. But I'm not American. Just to let you know. I'm *not* American. I want to find that Indian waitress in Toothpick's hometown and tell *her* I'm not American; I know she doesn't care, but I do, and I still feel like a fraud for letting her think otherwise this whole time. I don't mind when white people think I'm American (like I said, less potential for a racist encounter), but it makes me uncomfortable when I let another person of color assume as much, as though I am actively lying to them, or worse, actively hiding who I am.

Open any article on Aung San Suu Kyi, who is perhaps the most famous Myanmar figure in the world, and it'll at least once draw attention to the fact that she speaks with a British—or more specifically, an Oxford English—accent. When she spoke at Westminster, one journalist pointed out that her English accent was "almost perfect," naturally the result of the fact that she was married to an Englishman and lived in Oxford for an extended period of time. In preparation for her role as

Aung San Suu Kyi in the 2011 film *The Lady*, Michelle Yeoh hired an English tutor to help her perfect her character's accent. By now, the whole world knows that Aung San Suu Kyi speaks with an Oxford English accent, and yet it is still emphasized again and again, always brought up like a peculiarity or a fun fact about her, and as a result, so is the fact that she spent many of her formative years abroad in England. While she may be the daughter of the great General Aung San, who fought to liberate Burma from the British and paid for it with his life, she still attended college abroad—and at Oxford, no less— and married a British man. And even after spending a total of fifteen years in house arrest, during which she wasn't allowed any contact with her family, she never managed to lose her English accent. It's not just that she speaks fluent English, but that she speaks it with a posh English accent, and in doing so, as Marson says, "morph[s] into a different person," namely, someone who isn't Myanmar, not *really*. The journalists and analysts and biographers cannot call her British Myanmar because she is technically not, but they can imply it very, very heavily—and they never hesitate to do so.

There's this thing called foreign accent syndrome with which only about a hundred people worldwide have ever been diagnosed; following a stroke or head injury, these people have recovered and begun speaking in an accent different from the one they grew up speaking.

Your brain suffers a trauma, and just like that, your mouth is rewired in a whole new way. As someone who works in the arts, where everything is subjective, I've always found that science has the wonderful ability to simplify existential crises into objective and observable processes: death is just matter being destroyed; love is just a chemical imbalance in your brain; an accent is just how your tongue and lip and jaw move when you speak.

Because that's all it boils down to—you just have to train certain parts of your body to move in certain directions. When I was around five, I became obsessed with trying to make my tongue stand up on its side. One of my teachers showed me that she could do it, and I was intent on being able to do it as well. Every moment that I had no homework or chores to do, I focused on making my horizontal tongue vertical. And then one day after school, while I sat in the car in our school parking lot, it all happened so fast—one second my tongue refused to be anything but flat, and then the next it was up on its side and I could roll it around like a jump rope between my teeth. It's always baffled me that I remember this singular, silly moment of me just sitting in the back seat of my parents' car; I recall so clearly the joy I felt when I realized I had trained my body to do something it could not, or is not supposed to, do.

Margaret Thatcher's voice was deemed too shrill for a politician, and so she took voice lessons to lower her pitch and learn how to speak in a "calm, authoritative tone." I know a Myanmar woman who does professional hosting gigs, and when she speaks in English, she does so with a British accent; a friend once told me that she was specifically trained to speak like that, that her father made her take voice lessons so that she would sound British and book more gigs. (It worked.)

When I had to pick a foreign language to learn in middle school, the only real choice was always French, due to the fact that my mother is fluent in French.

"You're so lucky!" my French teacher said to us at our first parent-teacher conference after Mom revealed to him that she spoke French. "You can practice with someone who speaks French like a native speaker any time you want! Don't take that for granted, Pyae Pyae."

Every time we practiced at home, though, Mom would be disappointed and a little angry at me for not being able to pronounce a guttural *r*.

"F*rr*ahnçais," she would say.

"Français," I would repeat.

"Fai*rr*e."

"Faire."

"No. It has to come from the back of your throat. F*rr*."

"Furrr."

She told me about how, when she first started learning the language, she spent hours practicing that one consonant again and again until she got it right.

So *I* would sit in my bed each night, trying to perfect a guttural *r*. I wasn't sure of how long it would take me, but I kept telling myself that if I could teach my tongue to bounce around for fun, then I could teach my uvula and windpipe to do this; I could be my own accent clinician and train myself to say *frrançais* like my mother did. It didn't matter if my vocabulary and grammar was otherwise perfect. I wanted to speak French like a real French person, and to speak it without an accent. No, I wanted to speak it *with* a French accent. I never considered that maybe my tongue wasn't supposed to know how to do that. After all, if Mom could do it, then I could, too. I could speak like a native Frenchwoman, too.

When I'm speaking English in my American accent, I say *phone* as it should be, with the *ph* that sounds like an *f*; when I'm speaking to a Myanmar person, I don my Myanmar accent, and pronounce it without the *h* so that it's just "pone," because we don't have the *f* sound in our language. Because that's how Myanmar people talk, and I am Myanmar, not American. It's a small, weird thing, but when I'm talking to other Myanmar people, I don't want them to be so cognizant of my accent. Again, I recognize that it's an immense privilege, but I feel embarrassed that I so naturally developed something that should be unnatural in my mouth. A friend of a friend spent a couple of years in London and returned home with an obnoxious British accent; he didn't just pick up a few phrases or words here and there, but now exclusively spoke English with that accent. "It's clearly fake! He's so pretentious!" my friends and I whispered behind his back. But I am terrified that that's what people will say about me behind my back.

I used to think that I didn't know which was my real accent anymore, but the truth is that I know it's the American one, and I'm just too embarrassed to admit it. How come I managed to climb to the top of the accent social hierarchy without even trying to? Part of me wonders if I could train myself to transition into a Myanmar accent, although I know everyone would gasp at the thought—why get rid of something that secured me good jobs and, in general, respect? I was taught that speaking English with a Myanmar accent was embarrassing and indicated some sort of class and educational failure on my part, but what if this whole time, the opposite was true? There's a boldness in the assertion that you can speak the language of your colonizers but distinctly with your own accent, that you can take their words and literally twist them with your tongue to make them your own. When Chadwick Boseman was establishing his character for *Black Panther*, he worked with a dialect coach to perfect T'Challa's Xhosa accent. When Marvel executives tried pushing back, Boseman asked, "If we lose this right now, what else are we gonna throw away for the sake of making people feel comfortable?"

To him, it didn't make sense for the people of a nation who have proudly and explicitly never been colonized to speak and lead with a European accent. He felt that to speak with a European accent would be to convey "a white supremacist idea of what being educated is and what being royal or presidential is." I agree, and yet, if tomorrow I were presented with the opportunity to be just as fluent in English as I am now, minus the American accent, I know I wouldn't take it, and I also know there's a lot of internalized racism here that still needs processing.

In kids' animated TV shows, villains are almost always given foreign (i.e., non-American) accents, and in general, non-white characters almost always speak with their respective non-white accents, even though most voice actors are actually white (we don't even get hired to do the "Asian" accents!). In his documentary *The Problem with Apu*, Hari Kondabolu describes Apu's accent as "a white guy doing an impression of a white guy doing an impression of my father." I have never seen a Myanmar character in a Western animated show, but I wonder what kind of accent they would have. I wonder who would be hired to voice them. I wonder if the producers would know that, actually, Myanmar has 135 distinct ethnic groups, and that there are significant differences in accents within the country. Kachin people speak the Bamar language very differently from how Bamar people do, but would that even really matter to a team of white Hollywood producers? When I first moved to England, people were very quick to point out that different parts of the country had very distinct accents, Brummies sounded different from Scouses who sounded different from posh Etonians, I was told. But when it came to Asia, a lot of these same people suddenly seemed to think we all had the same accent; you know the one, with the slight pauses between each over-enunciated syllable—"How you do?" "I no speak English." "Where you come from?" When people ask me to do a Myanmar accent, I ask them what they think a Myanmar accent sounds like, and they sheepishly say, "I don't know, like, a Chinese one?" But shame on me for thinking that all Brits sound the same.

Remember that standing tongue that I mastered in the back of a car one day? It's now my go-to party trick. "Wow, how do you do that?" people exclaim when I open my mouth and swish it around. I smile and shrug. It was just a thing I practiced as a kid.

"It's so weird!"

Yes, I guess it is. I guess tongues aren't supposed to know how to do that.

PAPERWORK

Mom often says that I am going to break my father's heart one day.

Dad has always made it clear that he would never approve of my siblings and me marrying partners who weren't Myanmar. "How would I face people?" was what he told my mom, who told us. This is the kind of tired stereotypical Asian dad shit you see in movies, except the father acquiesces and approves in the end, which I also know Dad would never do.

I've had two boyfriends my entire life. While introducing either of them to my father would've been near-unthinkable if they were Myanmar men, the fact that my ex was white, as is Toothpick, means that Dad and I would rather go our whole lives pretending I will be single until the day I die, rather than address the fact that I am not only actively dating, but dating a white man. I consider myself to be a self-sufficient feminist, and yet I cannot think of any sentence that I am more petrified to utter than "Hello Father, please meet my Caucasian partner" as I gesture at Toothpick from head to toe like he's a prize on a quiz show.

In the six-plus years that we've been together, Toothpick and I have only ever lived in the same city for a month. We first started dating when I studied in Oxford for my junior year abroad and he still lived in his hometown in another part of England, where we were separated by a bus ride, a few stops on the London Tube, and a train ride. After my year abroad ended, I flew back to the United States to finish my last year of college, and then moved to London to do my MA; he moved to London shortly after I had finished my MA and already moved back to Yangon. It was some real star-crossed-lovers-wrong-place-right-time-right-place-wrong-time crap, but we were in love and happy. A couple of years after I left England, I moved to Norwich for a year to do another MA, and we became regulars on the Greater Anglia service between Norwich and London. In the time we've been dating, he's visited me twice in Yangon, but overall, I really think we have a shot at setting the world record for the largest percentage of conversations in a romantic relationship that take place over FaceTime.

Dad met Toothpick on his first trip to Myanmar when Toothpick had insisted on visiting Nay Pyi Taw, where Dad was posted, and we spent one night there; I think Dad knew that Toothpick was my boyfriend, but I would've rather voluntarily choked on the spaghetti I ordered at dinner than show any form of PDA in front of my father or gaze at Toothpick for longer than two seconds. It was an unspoken understanding that this white man at the table was a friend who was visiting from England.

My dad was born and raised in Myanmar, received a public Myanmar education, and joined the Myanmar military as early as he could. The concept of "racial purity" is openly taught in the Myanmar public school system. In 2015, the Buddhist Women's Special Marriage Law passed in parliament with a vote of 524 to 44 (with 8 abstentions). Under the law, the local township registrar is permitted to publicly display for two weeks a marriage application between a non-Buddhist man and a Buddhist woman (the idea being that to be truly Bamar automatically means being Buddhist), invite anyone who might have objections to voice their concerns, and potentially even take it to local court; think of the "If anyone has any objections, speak now or forever hold your peace" bit at a wedding, but instead of wedding guests, you're inviting any individual in your entire neighborhood to speak now. *Joke's on all of them, Dad included*, I used to think, *because fuck marriage.*

When we were children, Khin and I would argue over who would get to have *the* beach wedding. Obviously only one of us could have a beach wedding, because whoever did it second would've *obviously* been copying the first. I couldn't decide what kind of dress silhouette I wanted to wear: backless was sexy, but I began to develop back acne in my early teens; mermaid would've been too on-the-nose for a beach wedding; and sweetheart was a classic, but my chest got cold easily and I worried about all those people seeing my armpit fat. I used to be so obsessed with my theoretical wedding that I never considered what I wanted out of a marriage. As I slowly reached the age where people I went to school with were announcing their engagements on Facebook, I also became increasingly aware of the fact that my own attitude toward marriage was lukewarm at best. "Hey, would you marry me one day?" I'd ask Toothpick from time to time, and he'd shrug and say yes, and I'd shrug and nod, and that would be the end of our conversation. I thought hearing more of my friends' proposal stories would make me crave my own Instagram-worthy proposal one day as well. But after also hearing the same people's stories about marriage, I became disillusioned. It no longer appeared to be a sacred bond—it looked like just a bureaucratic necessity. Apart from a few outliers, in all the stories I heard, marriage was, at best, boring; a good marriage was one in which there was little to no drama, maybe a few white lies here and there, but overall, there were very few shouting matches. I am a romantic, but I'm not naïve. There's a reason the phrase *honeymoon phase* was coined. And apart from the distance thing and lack of an official marriage certificate, I now view Toothpick as a partner and not just a boyfriend, and in truth, have kind of felt married to him for a long time.

From the beginning of our relationship, he'd always said that he'd get married if his partner really wanted to, but it wasn't a goal for him. I used to roll my eyes and insist, "Well, *I* still want a nice engagement ring," and browse the Tiffany's online catalog and pretend I had a preference when it came to diamond cuts. Until one day, I realized I didn't want that future anymore, not really. By the time I found myself repeatedly circling back to the conclusion that it was just a piece of paper, my stupid, wise partner had influenced my opinions on a lot of other things as well, regardless of whether I *wanted* to be influenced—I'm more passionate about politics, I try to be more empathetic, I put things back where I found them in a store instead of placing them on the nearest rack. And, I guess, I no longer mind living a life of sin and raising our pets as bastards.

But in the real world—the racist, bureaucratic one we live in—we both know that the truth is we can't afford to be so anti-institutional. We can say we'll get married if we *have* to, but, well, at one point, we *will* have to.

When people listen to us complain about how expensive flights are and how much we miss each other, they ask why we don't just get married. Once, Toothpick came back from a night out where, after a few drinks, his friend Carl had asked if we were going to do long-distance again soon and then joked, "You guys should just get married so she can get British citizenship." He mentioned it to me in passing and laughed it off, but I had a weird lump in my throat. I wanted to cry, I didn't know why. I thought about it all through the next day and the next night, and I knew I would be thinking about it for a long time if I didn't bring it up.

"So, about what Carl said last night," I began. "About us getting married."

"Mmhmm?"

"It just made me . . . uncomfortable," I tried to explain.

"I'm sorry," he said, as he always does when I am sad or angry, even though he can't really understand why I'm sad or angry but still feels bad to see me upset nonetheless.

I started to cry. "I'm sorry," I blubbered and hiccupped. "I know he didn't mean it in a bad way. But I'm just always paranoid that that's what people think when they see us, and I just didn't think that someone I thought was our friend would also think that."

"I can bring it up with him the next time I see him if you want—" he offered, but I stopped him. I didn't want him to do that. I just wanted him to know.

I think about the comment now, though, and it still makes me want to cry. And it makes me want to cry whenever someone suggests that the best and easiest solution for us would be to simply get married, which, over the course of six-plus years, has been *a lot.*

For a long time, I thought marriage would be dull and boring, but after looking into it, it became clear that the actual act of marrying Toothpick would be anything but that. And that's precisely why I don't want to do it. "I don't want to deal with all the paperwork," I've started saying when asked if we're going to get married. My two biggest fears in the world are being buried alive and turtles, but for Toothpick, I would let myself be locked inside of a coffin for an hour while a giant turtle sat on my chest—but as a full-time freelancer, I draw the line at more paperwork.

The United Kingdom government has this thing called a Marriage Visitor visa. Isn't that strange—that you're labeled as a visitor in the country of the person with whom you're planning on spending the rest of your life? Every once in a while, when I'm bored and feel like I want a change more drastic than a nose ring, I google "U.K. marriage visa." The government page that it leads to is so long, however, and has so many words that I just skim it all and close the tab. It's too much paperwork.

There's an episode of *Modern Family* that made me cry the first time I saw it, and that I still think about. Gloria, who is a Colombian citizen, is studying for the American citizenship test and is excited about it until she finds out that the reason Jay, her American husband, is so supportive is because he hates waiting in the long non-citizen customs and immigration line whenever they return from holiday. Gloria gets mad and yells, "That son of a bitch wants me to turn my back on my homeland for an airport line?" Later, when Gloria confronts Jay about his motivations, he confesses that she's right, but goes on to explain, "When you and I come back to the country, we have to wait in separate lines like we're not even from the same family."

During my last stay in London, I used airline miles to book a few nights in a fancy hotel in Shoreditch. After a day spent wandering around the city, Toothpick and I came back to the hotel and took photos in the overpriced photo booth in the lobby, then we hung out on one of the couches in the bar and alternated between making out and talking about politics or Taylor Swift; we'd been together for five and a half years, but on that particular night, it felt like we were lovestruck teenagers on their first unchaperoned date, and I wanted so badly to have many more blurry days and nights like that, minus the looming knowledge that I was going to get on a flight in a couple of days before my visa ran out. So later that night, while I was still riding that high of dizzying love and overpriced Shoreditch pizza, I forced myself to read through all the requirements that I needed to meet in order to apply for a marriage visa before we got married, making mental notes under each point. I tried to be practical about it, like I was checking things off of my shopping list. The page stated:

You must prove that you're:

- 18 or over
- free to give notice of marriage, to marry or enter into a civil partnership in the UK within 6 months of your arrival
- in a genuine relationship
- visiting the UK for less than 6 months
- leaving the UK at the end of your visit
- able to support yourself without working or help from public funds, or that you can be supported and housed by relatives or friends
- able to meet the cost of the return or onward journey

After some more research, I learned that, alternatively, we could get married first and then I could apply for a Family visa, which would allow me to stay in the country for two and a half years before I needed to apply for an extension. I made a note of the cost of the visas alone, which would run into thousands of pounds, if not tens of thousands, over however many years it took before I needed to stop applying for them. Then there were the various fees and surcharges I'd have to pay, the time we'd both need to take off work to go to visa centers, along with the train costs, photocopy costs, translation costs—it went on and on and on and on.

I took a deep breath and moved on to the next page. *Just a shopping list, just keep ticking the boxes*, I repeated in my head. If we felt just bold enough and did go through with the process, the documents that we—and by *we*, I mean *I*, because let's be honest here, it's really *me* and my brown skin and passport that's being scrutinized— would need to provide in order to prove the above points for either a Spousal or a Family visa would include:

- a current passport or other valid travel identification
- proof of your future plans for the relationship, for example documents to show where you'll live
- details of where you intend to stay and your travel plans
- details of the marriage or civil partnership and proof that you've paid money for some of its costs
- proof that you're planning to get married in the UK, for example a booking confirmation or emails between you and the venue
- a good knowledge of English

While Toothpick was in the bathroom, I slammed my laptop shut and sobbed alone in bed. I felt stupid crying while reading a government website, but it was all too much. I grew up being told by books and movies written by white people that getting married only required falling in love. It now makes a lot of sense that the romantic comedies I grew up watching almost exclusively starred American or European characters—I don't think *The Prince and Me* would've had the same punch if Julia Stiles had to wait three to six weeks for her visa to get approved before she hopped on a plane and put everything on the line.

I have about four boxes in my home office that, to date, contain six years' worth of train tickets, cinema tickets, arcade tickets, overpriced photo booth strips, festival wristbands, concert stubs, Polaroid pictures, birthday cards, Valentine's Day cards, just because cards, stickers, holiday souvenirs, bowling scorecards, and tour bus passes. I've kept it all because I am a senti-mentalist, a hoarder, and a romantic—but if a fire broke out, while I would think for a few seconds about salvaging these boxes, ultimately, I'd let them go. *Don't worry about the mementos*, I'd scold myself. *Your relationship isn't any less strong without them. It's all just paper.*

So what is it that turns paper into paper*work*? Without even meaning to, I have kept a meticulous paper trail of our relationship. Now that we've begun realistically talking about getting married one day, those faded pieces of paper that I keep in those boxes are so valuable that I wonder if I should make digital scans of all of them and upload them onto Dropbox as well as onto five different USB sticks that I keep in different locations around the city, like they're some super top-secret government agency files. Every time I declutter my office and I think of throwing away a movie stub or a concert wristband, I practice this hypothetical interview in my head and the confident, specific answers that I'll give as I flip through my files. "This is a ticket from when we went to see *Hamilton*, the first time, anyway." "This is the score-card from when we played minigolf for his twenty-ninth birthday." "These are the arcade tickets I won at the Brighton Pier on our first holiday together." It's a strange shift that I didn't even realize had taken place as our relationship got more serious—at some point, these stubs and tickets and photos went from being sweet mementos that happened to be pieces of paper, to the only concrete proof I had that our relationship was real and genuine. Toothpick can afford to throw away all of his festival wristbands and the tickets from when we went to see all of the *Avengers* movies, but I can't.

I believe that visas and borders, in general, prey on the poor and the vulnerable, and should be entirely abolished, and I think that forcing two married people to submit a huge stack of documents like they're applying for a job simply because one person was born on the wrong side of a man-made line in the sand is nothing short of cruel. Looking through that list, the criterion that hurts the most is having to prove that we're "in a genuine relationship," and the knowledge that he wouldn't have to do any of this if he were marrying a nice British girl with an uncomplicated British passport. You can show travel itineraries and birth certificates and bank statements for all the other points, but proving that a relationship is *genuine*? How does anyone do that? And then there are times where I wonder if all of this effort is even worth it. Maybe we'll get the flimsy piece of paper saying we're legally married and we still won't be seen as a real family. Because what if we went through all that—we got married and we filed all the paperwork and we paid the thousands of pounds in visa fees and we meticulously kept track of all of my visa reapplication appointments until I was finally granted citizenship—and the looks and casual remarks still stuck around? The jokes still wouldn't end, and some people wouldn't be joking. I would be accused of having married him because I wanted a different, more powerful passport, because I wanted to abuse the NHS, because I wanted a white-sounding last name. I don't want to be "the Asian wife"; I know I shouldn't care if his racist friends and relatives and colleagues say they know a guy who brought home a wife from Asia, but I know I still will, even if just a tiny bit.

Celeste Ng once wrote in an article for *The Cut* about online Asian male communities that identify and harass Asian women who marry non-Asian men: "The men who harass me know three things: I'm Chinese American, my husband is white, and our son is multiracial. *You hate Asian men*, they insist; *you hate your own child. You hate yourself.*" I am terrified that if I marry Toothpick, I will be on the receiving end of the kind of derogatory language that Ng mentions, that I'll be accused of white-worshipping, or holding a colonial mentality, or of being a self-hating Asian woman. I'm terrified that I'll be seen as looking down on Asian culture, as hating Asian men, as upholding white supremacy—all under the guise of *love*; I'm terrified that I will be accused of these things by my own family, by my own father. I would be a lot less scared and a lot more indifferent toward what all the white people thought of me if I knew I had my family in my corner. Mom has a particular phrase for whenever I say something that glorifies the West or an aspect of Western culture: bo kyet chee, or "foreign chicken shit."

I could not care less about Toothpick's passport, but I get why others would think differently. I can't ignore the imbalance of power in our relationship, not only when we compare the color of our forearms, but also when we take out our passports at the airport. At the end of a holiday in Berlin a couple of years ago, we had a fight at the airport while we were waiting for our flight back to London. I don't remember what we were arguing about, but at the time it seemed big, and I refused to talk to Toothpick as we made our way to the boarding gate. Before we could enter the waiting area at the gate, there were two counters staffed by a couple of immigration officers who were checking passports to make sure people had the right paperwork. Toothpick walked up to the counter on the right and I to the left. We both knew what was going to happen. His guy took one look at the front page of his passport and waved him through. Mine looked at my photo, at my face, at my photo again, at my passport cover, flipped through the pages to locate my Schengen visa, looked at my British permanent residence card, and at me again. I felt bad for the people behind me, who were rolling their eyes at having picked the wrong queue while everyone in the right-side queue breezed through. I was still annoyed from our fight, but I tried not to fidget, and I definitely tried not to notice all the white people passing me by who were examining me to see what it was about me and my passport that seemed suspicious.

It doesn't get any less tedious or embarrassing regardless of how many times we do this. We love going on holiday together, but whenever we land at the airport in London, Toothpick heads over to the automated gates while I join the non-EU customs and immigration line. "See you on the other side," we always say before we kiss and go our separate ways. And each time, a small part of me worries that I'll get called over and detained in an office and for some reason, in the absolute worst-case scenario, I don't get allowed back into the country and I don't see him on the other side. Maybe it would be worth getting married and going through all that paperwork if it meant we could stop separating at airports. Maybe Jay had a point.

If I ever talked all of this through with my father, he'd no doubt laugh and say, "All of this for a man? A white man? Look at you—you're so smart and funny and beautiful! You could have any Myanmar man you wanted!" A few years ago, Dad was approved by his work to go to Hawaii for a little over a month; this was one of just a handful of times that he'd left the country in his entire life, and also his first trip to the United States. Upon returning, he said Hawaii was great, and that his favorite thing that he encountered there was Costco ("You can just buy things, use them, and then return it if you change your mind!"). I envy passports that would allow me to impulsively purchase a ticket to almost any country in the world, but Dad is more than satisfied with going on short trips here and there, all the while never forgetting where he comes from. As great as Costco's return policy was, it wasn't enough to change my dad's mind on the fact that he is a proud Myanmar man who could never consider another country his home. On his second trip to the United States, and his first and only one to New York City, we took a tour of the United Nations Headquarters, and in the section of the lobby where they have framed portraits of past secretaries-general, he made me take photos of him standing proudly in front of the picture of U Thant.

Despite what my parents, especially my father, would say, *of course* I feel ashamed every time I consider replacing my passport with another, seemingly better one. When Mom found out that my uncle and his wife and two children had given up their Myanmar passports and were now officially (and exclusively) Singapore citizens, she tutted, "I don't even know when he did it! He didn't tell any of us!" The Myanmar government doesn't allow dual citizenship, and so if I were to marry Toothpick, I'd have to choose: be a visitor in his country, or in mine. Objectively, it's a no-brainer. Passport privilege is a real thing. A British passport has a mobility score of 113, meaning that someone who holds one can dip in and out of 113 countries; a Myanmar passport has a mobility score of 36. Toothpick is almost always exempt from visas; the only country for which he has had to apply for one is Myanmar. When two couple friends of ours told us about how for the woman's most recent birthday, the guy told her to pack a bag and then surprised her with a trip to Paris, I was simultaneously happy and envious because I knew *we* could never do that, that Toothpick could never surprise me with a trip to a random country without having to make sure I was legally allowed to even travel there.

Until recently, it had never crossed my mind that there could be a version of my future in which I'd have to apply for a visa myself to enter Myanmar. How would I even face the immigration officer? What would I say if they asked why I was coming as a tourist to the country that my father has spent the majority of his adult life serving and protecting? Would I just answer in English so they'd at least think I was born abroad, and with this passport, as opposed to voluntarily switching to it? I try to remind myself that what it says on the front page of my passport would never be able to nullify the fact that I am Myanmar, but it would still say *a lot*. I've never met anyone who loves this country more than my father, and I cannot fathom the disappointment he would feel to have a daughter who went through so much trouble and paperwork in order to willingly renounce her citizenship, the same one he proudly maintains.

Dad hates showing emotion, and while I can be sappy and sentimental in certain situations, he and I have nurtured a strong but silent love over the years, in spite of his being gone for long periods of time when I was growing up. But I remember one night when I was twelve or thirteen, and I was still awake in bed when I heard the connecting door between my and Shan's room creak open. By then, I'd perfected my nightly routine of flipping onto my right side so that my back was to the door, pulling up my blanket, and shoving my phone under my spare pillow—all in under the two seconds it took for Mom to fully open the door and check if I was asleep. That night, I shut my eyes and stayed statuesque as usual, aware that Mom was still standing there in the doorway, except it wasn't Mom this time. I know my father's breathing even from several feet away, as well as his silence, probably because we are both very good at being silent and do it often, and I knew then, even without hearing him or smelling his scent or feeling his hands brush my hair out of my face, that he had come home early to surprise us and was now standing there and smiling at the sight of me tucked in bed. To this day, I can still feel his presence when he's entered the same room as me (I don't even have to turn around); I can't bear the thought of losing that presence.

When I was in college, every time Dad and I talked on the phone, it wouldn't last more than one minute; this seemed weird to me at first, so I began checking the call log when we hung up, and each time, it was true—we'd said goodbye before the call hit the one-minute mark. And that was fine. We were just always able to say everything we needed to say in under sixty seconds. Even when he called me on my birthday, we'd still keep the call under a minute because apart from "happy birthday" and "I love you," what else could he have to say? His gift to me was efficiency, and I loved him for it. He can't bear the thought of me disliking him, would go to the ends of the universe and back five times over for me, thinks that I'm capable of navigating a rocket ship if I wanted to. As a way to thank him, I try my hardest to not ever upset him, which is perhaps also why we've always done well with our minute-long phone calls. It is near-impossible to argue—or, say, bring up the fact that I have a boy-friend now—during a conversation that lasts less than sixty seconds.

Sometimes I find comfort in pretending that my dad is so against me marrying someone who isn't Myanmar and Buddhist because he doesn't want to see me get hurt. Maybe Dad is more scared of what others would say about me (and possibly *to* me) if he let me marry some-one who wouldn't necessarily ever fit in, and so shutting it down completely is the way to go. We know Myanmar women who have married white men, and we've heard all the comments from both Myanmar and non-Myanmar friends: "She married him because he buys her expensive purses and all she has to do is be pretty." "She married him because she wants to move to Europe." "She mar-ried him because he's old and has a lot of money." Dad thinks that I could have any man I wanted—even though personally he'll never think anyone is good enough for me—so why put myself through all of this for this one particular man? There will be others, a long line of them queuing down the street. I know my father loves me, and when you do something out of love, can it ever really be the wrong decision? If you are a Myanmar citizen flying out of Myanmar, you have to write down your father's name and national registration card number at the top of the Immigration Departure Card—what would I do if the last time I flew out of Myanmar to go settle down in another country, I found myself disowned and didn't really have a father whose name and NRC number I could write down?

I didn't confess to Toothpick for a very long time that my parents would never support any potential marriage between us; I felt like it would've made him sad and powerless because the problem was something he obviously couldn't change. After all, it would make me sad, too, if the roles were reversed and my partner told me that he would essentially have to choose between me and his parents. Sometimes, the selfish, cowardly part of me wonders if my relationship will just implode and the universe will have made the choice for me. I can be difficult and unreasonable at times, and sometimes when Toothpick and I are in the middle of a very bad fight and I'm screaming terrible things at him, I think, "This is it, this is why he leaves me." But he never does, and there are times when that doesn't provide the kind of relief that it should.

"What would you do if your parents didn't approve of us getting married because I wasn't white?" I asked Toothpick out loud once, about five years into our relationship.

With zero hesitation or second thought, he responded, "I'd tell them to fuck off." While I was glad to be reminded that he had my back no matter what, I was also mad at him for always sticking to his morals. Damn him for knowing the right thing to do, and more importantly, for having the guts to follow through. Why couldn't he be the one stuck with the impossible nationalist father?

I wonder if anyone has pointed out to all the Myanmar nationalists that this concept of blood and racial purity was actually inherited from British colonialists who feared that interracial marriages would fuck with their preestablished racial hierarchy. Blurred racial lineages are not conducive to European racial purity or superiority; what do you do with a half-Brown, half-white child if the status quo is that white people are superior to Brown people? Oh, the irony of it all, now that I, a Brown Myanmar woman, have a white, specifically British, boyfriend. I bet our ancestors are rolling in their graves. Some people think that I haven't married Toothpick because I'm scared of my father's opinion. But I'm not scared, just sad. I don't want to spend the rest of our lives sitting through dinners where I pretend that my partner is nothing more than a good, platonic friend; I want our silence to be the result of a warm comfort, not borne out of a fear of stepping on a particularly loud eggshell. I want Dad to like Toothpick, to see the way I do how funny and kind and wonderful he is; for two people who are so alike in a lot of ways, it kills me that *this* is one of the few things that Dad and I don't agree on. I know it's asking a lot to expect my father to actively view my partner as his son—and it's okay if he can never fully bring himself to do so, it really is—but I don't want to stop being his daughter. That would be a lot of paperwork to sort through.

Toothpick and I broke up forty-eight days short of our seven-year anniversary. Toward the end, I held on to this unfounded yet recurring hope that if we just held on until we made it to seven years, then as a "reward" for reaching the lucky seven milestone, we would find a way to work things out. But then one morning I went over to Khin's house, and, curled up on one side of her lime green couch, I told her and Poe, "I think we're breaking up." And I knew that was it. Before I even finished saying the sentence, I knew that I had made up my mind.

It turns out in the end I couldn't do it. I couldn't move to another country, another city, where, exclusively on paper, but nonetheless for a very long time, all I would be was a spouse, a wife. I don't see marriage ever being a goal for me in a relationship, but it was the bureaucratic requirement of marriage that I couldn't live with. I could've lived with being a wife if that was important to him, and especially if I could be *his* wife, but not under those circumstances. I know in my heart and in my mind that I would have also been a lot of other things, but whenever someone new would ask me why I'd moved, the only honest answer would be "Because my husband lives here," and that was something I just couldn't give in to, if *give in to* even is the correct phrase. Is that just me being too proud? Maybe. But I did not want to wake up every day for days, weeks, months, maybe even years in a row with the knowledge that I was there on a marriage visa. I didn't even want to imagine what we would've done if one day Toothpick was fired and he struggled to find a new job, and how we would've reacted if all of that stress was further exacerbated by the knowledge that I would have to leave if he could not find a job that paid him a certain minimum salary, and quickly.

I explained all of this to Poe and Khin, who listened and, as shocked as they were by my seemingly sudden epiphany, did not try to dissuade me. Khin said that the mere act of having to prove that a marriage was legitimate was so "dehumanizing." I was stunned by her accuracy, and also relieved by the confirmation. I'd spent the months prior trying to convince myself that I would be happy living in England because I would be with him, but it took a lot of mental gymnastics, none of which quite landed perfectly. I would remind myself of all the Myanmar women I knew who'd moved abroad to marry and start families with their white partners, and I'd spend hours scrolling through their Facebook photos and trying to tell myself that I, too, could be as happy as they were, if only I took that initial leap of faith. But Khin was right—I know myself, and I know I would've been furious and probably humiliated throughout the whole process of trying to prove again and again that our relationship was legitimate.

"Why don't you try changing your frame of thinking?" Khin suggested as she watched me agonize over having to break things off. "Maybe don't think of it as you moving for *him*, but instead as you moving for *yourself*. You're moving for *your* happiness, so *you* can be with him." Because that was the heart of it all, wasn't it? Whichever one of us moved, it would've felt like a sacrifice for that person. Whenever I thought about marrying him and moving to London, all I could concentrate on was what I would be giving up: my family, my friends, my apartment, my passport, my citizenship—in essence, my whole identity.

During our last call, our Breakup Call, as I've creatively come to deem it, I kept trying to explain my feelings over and over to him through so much snot and so many tears. "I keep saying to myself, *But if we lived in the same country, there wouldn't be anything else wrong with us that we couldn't work through.*" I cried, and he would nod, and through *his* tears and snot, say, "I know." Because we knew. We always knew. We knew that if we ever broke up, this would be why.

"I kept telling myself that all that mattered was how much we loved each other, and then everything else would work out in the end. I just thought that the fact that we loved each other would be enough," I continued.

"I know. But it's not. That's not how it works, Pyae," I remember him saying with a sad smile that made me come *this close* to immediately taking back everything I'd just said and begging him to think of another way that we could make this work.

Is it naïve to admit that I thought love would prevail in the end? I know it's definitely cheesy. He and I would often rant about the fact that borders are entirely manmade, and that the existence of things like passports and visas and immigration laws hinge entirely on a wider societal belief in these imaginary lines in the earth; so now, it feels almost shameful to admit that, in the end, we were so attached to the relationships and communities we'd built within these imaginary lines that neither one of us could bring ourselves to move from within one set of lines to another. Neither of us are even particularly patriotic individuals—he hates the monarchy! I couldn't sing the Myanmar national anthem if you put a gun to my head!—but it turns out that unbeknownst to ourselves, we had roots that were firmly planted in the soils on which we were born, more firmly than either of us thought they were. It also feels embarrassing to say that they won in the end, although I'm still trying to figure out who this *they* is that I find myself cursing at in the middle of the night. When I told Mom that we broke up, she asked me what happened, and I shrugged and gave her the truth, which was that nothing *happened*. There was no fight, no infidelity, no committal of an unforgivable act on either of our parts; and despite it being my biggest fear, it wasn't even because Dad never approved of, or even accepted, our relationship.

"What are you going to do with all the bits about me in your book?" Toothpick joked before we hung up on the Breakup Call.

I told him I wouldn't *do* anything, that all the good things that happened were—are—all true.

We just couldn't get our paperwork in order.

GOOD, MYANMAR, GIRL

t's long been a joke among my family that I have no friends. I promise you that this isn't entirely accurate (despite what they will *insist*); I do have friends, just not a lot of them, and not a lot of close ones. I'm almost always down to catch up with current and former colleagues and people I went to school with, but I also believe that there's a distinction between someone you know and have run into a few times here and there, and a friend. It's not necessarily that I'm guarded (I'm writing a book where I reveal secrets about my whole damn life!) or even arrogant enough to deem myself picky, but just that I'm glad to have learned early on the importance of finding your people in the world. Not every person I meet will be my people, and I'm more than fine with that—that's how it's supposed to be anyway.

It's weird, and more than a little concerning to my parents and grandparents, I'm sure, just how good I am at being alone, and I'm sure they worry about me being one of those old people who dies alone in their homes and aren't found until their neighbors notice a funky smell a week later. In my opinion, though, this is one of my biggest strengths, not to mention one of my favorite things about myself. I am good at eating alone in restaurants; at sitting in a packed cinema alone; at spending a whole day in my apartment without making physical contact with any other humans. I hated group projects in school, and I hate group chats that involve more than four members; in both scenarios, chaos reigns and nothing concrete ever gets accomplished. I know a lot of writers grumble that writing often feels like a solitary task, and while I get why that can be frustrating at times, I frequently say that that's one of the main reasons why I can't imagine myself being anything other than a writer.

I wasn't always like this, however. I used to hate being alone, especially as a shy, chubby teenager. In high school, my best friends and I would eat lunch together on the right side of the black-tiled steps outside the school building (the left side belonged to another group of girls). It became a sort of ritual at the start of every school year to let the new freshmen know that that specific spot was ours, and for the first couple of weeks, whichever one of us first got out of class would rush to the space and spread out their belongings, and stare down any group of young meat who sauntered over to eat there (we weren't mean, there just wasn't enough room for more than four to five people!). Whoever was holding down the fort would and could never be intimidated, because we knew backup would be arriving in mere minutes. On one afternoon, though, all three of my friends ended up having other prior engagements, and although each of them said they'd meet me at our spot once they were done, it still meant I would be on my own for at least the first twenty minutes of lunch. It was far enough into the school year that I no longer had to claim our territory, but still, I couldn't bear the pitiful looks that I was sure people would shoot in my direction as I ate lunch all alone in the spot big enough for four people. So I bought rice and pork curry from the cafeteria, shoved the white Styrofoam box with the flimsy plastic spoon into my messenger bag, and locked myself inside one of the toilet stalls in the girls' bathroom on the ground floor. Worried that the scent of the curry might start catching people's attention if I stayed in there too long, I gobbled down my food while sitting on the toilet seat cover, the whole time wondering if, in fact, eating my lunch in a toilet stall was less embarrassing than eating alone on the front steps of the school building.

But practice makes perfect, and once you move to a country where you don't have any family or a gang of best friends to eat lunch with every day (at least, not at first), you have no choice but to practice being alone a lot. But even after I did make friends, an unexpected shift in my thinking occurred, and the idea of doing things on my own began to feel more exciting than sad. Without my parents or grandmother or an auntie always fretting about me doing things on my own, I began to embrace that I was now allowed to venture out without anyone's company. It also came to my attention that in American society, people, and especially women, are actively encouraged to do things alone. Go on a solo trip around Europe! Attend a concert on your own! Eat alone at a restaurant! For a lot of my women friends, these things were checkboxes on some invisible feminist manifesto that they felt proud to tick off as they returned from their big summer adventures and exclaimed in exhilaration, "You *must* treat yourself to an expensive bottle of wine on a clifftop café overlooking the Mediterranean Sea!" or something like that. During her gap year, my friend Katie backpacked around the whole damn world on her own; I'm not quite as adventurous as Katie (and let's be honest, I probably never will be), but after moving to the land of the free and the home of the brave, I started to embrace my newfound freedom and feign bravery as I tried my hand at the smallest, stupidest things that I was told a teenage Myanmar girl should never do. I would buy a single ticket for the cinema, or put in my earphones and walk the two miles from the college campus to the town center on my own (to the utter horror of my mother when I told her on the phone at the end of the day), or savor my meal as I had lunch for one in a restaurant, and the more I did it, the less scary and embarrassing it felt.

When I moved back to Myanmar after years of solo grocery trips and midnight cinema viewings, though, the difference was instant and palpable. Here, Mom or a cousin insists that they'll join me, even if I'm seeing a film that they didn't know existed starring an actress they've never heard of. My parents' friends were shocked when they heard that my mother and father were letting me move out and live on my own; of course, I noticed that they weren't nearly as anxious when my brother did the same thing a few years later, despite the fact that you actually need a car to get to his place, whereas I'm a five-minute walk from my parents' house. I've never been able to go away to another city or town on a solo trip because, as everyone eagerly reminds me, "A good young Myanmar girl can't do that." And in the instances where I drown out Mom's comments and have a sit-down meal alone, I can't fully ignore the looks when I'm the only table of one that's clearly not waiting for a date to show up in Pizza Hut. "Sorry, I almost feel bad showing this to you," a server once joked as she showed me to a booth and handed me a menu for their current group meal promotions that featured photos of families laughing and bonding over slices of a large Chicken Deluxe.

Here, there must be something wrong with the woman in the corner who came on her own, who isn't part of a group, who doesn't even have *one other friend* to share a pizza pie with. What's wrong with that woman? Why is she eating alone? Whereas my American friends would tell me all about how empowering and feminist it was of me to wine and dine myself, here, I feel as though I just come across as lonely, and maybe a little sad.

I'm told that you can't go through life alone. Community plays a key role in surviving as a human. The story goes that when asked what she considered to be the first sign of civilization, the anthropologist Margaret Mead pointed to a fifteen-thousand-year-old human femur bone with a healed fracture that was found in an archaeological site. She said that in nature, a broken leg means death because you cannot run from danger or walk toward water or food. You become easy prey for predators. The healed bone in this case, though, suggested that this particular human had been protected and looked after, and their injury, tended to long enough for them to recover. Someone formed a connection with them and took them in—that is how communities are formed, and that is what communities do.

To be Myanmar is to be family-oriented. It never seemed strange to me that A May has six siblings; on the other hand, I had one friend in high school who was an only child, and we always asked her if it was weird not having any brothers or sisters, and found it peculiar that there were no siblings for us to greet whenever we went over to her house. Several of my American friends, though, are only children; I can't imagine how *quiet* such a house must be. Myanmar people have and want big families, and we love living in the same houses as our big families. I never quite understood my American or British friends' embarrassment over living at home with their parents; when I told them that I'd be moving back into my parents' house for a bit after graduation, I'd also feel the need to explain that I *prefer* to live alone because of the privacy, but I've never felt *embarrassed* at the thought of living at home with my parents. One family we're close with has all five adult children (three of whom are married, two with *their* own kids) still living under the same roof as their elderly parent. After all, the deal is that your parents shelter and look after you, and then later on, you do the same for them; at the same time, you also shelter and look after your own children so that when you get older, the cycle continues. The community grows.

In college, Noah and I would talk about becoming parents one day, and I said that I imagined having children by "Twenty-six, twenty-seven, maybe twenty-eight?" When you are seventeen, being twenty-six seems like such an adult age, and I knew that was how old Mom was when she had me, and roughly how old A May was when she had her first child. Noah, whose parents had him much later, was shocked. He confidently stated that neither of us would be even remotely ready to have a child by the time we were twenty-six or even twenty-eight. I hate inflating Noah's ego, but he was right, and by the time I hit my early twenties, I was laughing at naïve teenage-me who thought so highly of present-me and believed that I'd be ready for a child in just a few years' time.

I am very bad at being a woman, according to Mom. I realize that this is a weird—and honestly, maybe kind of hurtful—thing for a woman to hear from the lips of her own mother, but I've heard it so many times that it's stopped bothering me. Mom is so proud of my academic and professional accomplishments, but she also reminds me on a regular basis that I could and should be working toward being a better woman.

If you ask her, I think she'll say the first big indicator that things were going downhill was when, in the middle of my late teenage years, I decided that I didn't want to wear bras anymore. She'd hoped that my transition from a girl into a young woman would be smooth, but then, when I was about seventeen or eighteen, I just stopped wearing all of those pretty lace bras that I was once *desperate* to own as a wide-eyed fourteen-year-old. To this day, whenever the subject of my not wearing a bra comes up, my mother and her friends look at me with faces that cannot hide the horror and disappointment.

"They're going to sag in a few years' time, like an old woman," Mom says in an attempt to scare me, but it never works.

"I mean, it's not like I have much to try to hold up," I reply, smirking as I look down at my A-cups.

"Geez Pyae, you're a woman. A *young* Myanmar woman! Act like one!" she snaps.

Anyone who knows me knows that I'm not a big fan of babies or kids. I'm not mean to them, and I'll tolerate them if I must, but I'm not a "kid person." I've noticed that it's okay for boys and men to not want to be around kids (hello, men who refer to looking after their own goddamn child as "babysitting"), but people have literally shoved babies into my arms on more than one occasion without even asking if I want to hold said lump of flesh. Don't get me wrong—if and when my best friends make me their children's godmother, I will love and spoil the shit out of those little pink-cheeked fiends like nothing else you've ever seen, but I don't get why my uterus and I are expected to muster up that same reaction toward every single baby we encounter. If we're at a party and someone has brought their baby, I'm invited to come look and coo over the tiny bundle while my brother and father get to stay seated at the table and eat as they continue to talk about Man Things. At home, while sitting quietly at the dining table as Mom and A May exchanged gossip with their friends over coffee, I'd only ever hear of *men* who had happily chosen the bachelor life, and *men* who had disappeared on women they'd slept with once the latter had wound up accidentally pregnant; there was always a woman who was convinced she would be the one to convert her partner into dad material, or who had weathered the whispers and public shame and raised the child on her own. For most of my life, I was convinced that not wanting to be a parent was a semi-regular occurrence for boys and men, while the only thing every woman with a partner wanted was to become a mother. When Toothpick would tell people that he didn't really think kids were in his future, they'd nod breezily, never asking him why, but they did always ask what *I* thought about that and why *I* felt that way as well.

As a child, Shan had one of those baby toys that you could feed prepackaged sachets of food to that it would later poop out; I thought it was the creepiest thing I'd ever seen in a toy store, and I couldn't believe we'd brought it home with us. Fast-forward to a couple of years ago when Mom and I were buying a present for her friend's kid, and the saleswoman drew our attention to a similar, more advanced, pooping baby doll; it'd been over a decade since we bought that first one for Shan, but it seemed that the little monstrosities were still alive and well. The feminist in me gagged at the picture on the back of the box of a group of young girls excitedly feeding their dolls and changing their diapers, and I tried to suggest a cool Hot Wheels set or a simple board game instead. "Do you think this *child's* idea of fun will be to *look after a fake baby*?" I tried to argue with Mom to no avail, because at the cash register, the saleswoman and my mother both agreed that this would, in fact, be a great gift for a seven-year-old girl.

It now seems obvious that the only ever real option for me was to not have children, but before I could recognize that, I needed to expand my understanding of feminism and womanhood, and my understanding of myself not just as a woman, but specifically as a Myanmar woman, to arrive at a place where I was as confident in my identity as a cisgender woman as in my decision to never have children. It also helped that for the vast majority of this journey, I had a partner who encouraged me to ask these questions of myself, and who, in the end, landed on the same page as me. It's not insignificant that Toothpick was white and had bolted out of his parents' house as soon as he could afford to do so. In the context of Myanmar culture, you aren't really a family or even partners until you're married, but obviously with Toothpick, that wasn't the case. We *were* partners, and despite the opinion of Mom and A May and every other elder in my life whom I'd informed of our plans to never have kids, he and I viewed our child-free future not as a terrifyingly lonely expanse of time, but as an opportunity for us to come up with our own definitions of home and family (and to spend our lives doing as much stupid shit as we wanted without worrying about babysitters or college funds). Reflecting on it now, it would be disingenuous of me to not admit that part of the reason I was so self-assured and outspoken about my decision to be child-free, even at such a young age, was because I already knew that didn't automatically mean I would spend the rest of my life alone. I had a partner with whom I'd already planned out this exhilarating, diaper-free future—until, well, I didn't. I don't now.

There is a Myanmar term for old people who have been single for as long as their friends and family can remember, and who will probably remain single until they die: a pyo. Not coincidentally, this is also the same term for a virgin, and older individuals who fall in this category are called a pyo gyi: "old virgins." An a pyo gyi is someone who grows old without a partner or children of their own, and is content devoting their life to their job or to looking after their parents or to helping their siblings raise *their* children—but at the end of the day, they go to bed alone. Girls and young, unmarried women are often described as an a pyo lay ("young virgin"), and if they remain unmarried, they transition into an a pyo gyi.

I have tried to explain many times now that my plan isn't to be a fifty-year-old a pyo gyi. I am a romantic, I love dating, I love love, I love being a girlfriend. And still, I think about how if we had settled down in Myanmar, it would've been enough of a struggle to integrate Toothpick into our Myanmar family and larger community, and how that struggle would've been expounded by the fact that every time an auntie or uncle asked us, "So now that you're married, when are you having kids?" I would've replied "Never" through a polite grimace while squeezing Toothpick's hand as I imagined it to be the person's throat. I *get* why people don't believe me when I say I don't want children. After all, it goes against biology and the primal, evolutionary desire to preserve your lineage, doesn't it? For women, there is supposedly no stronger instinct than your maternal instinct to care for and protect your children; apparently, even seven-year-old girls love doing this with their toys! My mother has been a working parent our whole lives, the epitome of women-can-have-it-all-ism in my eyes, and proof that you can be a Myanmar woman with a family and a successful career. When older women tell me that I *should* want kids and insist that I *will* want them one day, I know they're not saying that that's *all* I'll do; they're just saying that alongside all the other great things that are in store for me, I'll also become a mother because that's part and parcel of inhabiting a female body.

The key to being comfortable being alone is giving yourself permission to enjoy being selfish—which, let's be honest, is an embarrassing personality trait to acknowledge. And while I believe that there's a very good reason you're supposed to put on your own oxygen mask before anyone else's, that's not what you do in a Myanmar community. Concepts such as "self-care" and "me time" are fully Western notions, and in Myanmar culture, they're generally viewed as over-the-top and, well, selfish. There is no space for alone time or me time when you're part of a community; Mom reminds me that you do not, and cannot, put your phone on Do Not Disturb while you're sleeping because what if someone from your community is trying to reach you for help? In *her* case, she sleeps with her phone beside her pillow in case one of us needs her in the middle of the night; I cannot imagine doing this, cannot imagine *wanting* to do this, for any human being.

I read a story years ago about a small tribe somewhere that lived in the depths of the forest for decades upon decades with no contact with the outside world, until one day, they ventured beyond their familiar territory. I've tried and failed to find a news article about this story and part of me is tempted to think I made it up, but I know I didn't because the bit that stuck with me is this: when this group was asked why after all this time, they finally decided to see what else was out there in the world, the reason wasn't a *what* but a *whom*—they had gotten lonely, and decided that whatever threats the outside world might pose were worth facing if there was a chance of connecting with other humans and expanding their community.

I am very good at being alone, so good in fact, that sometimes I forget that there is a difference between being alone and being lonely.

I'm never ashamed of my not wanting to be a mother, but sometimes I'm terrified that that means I'm setting myself up for a lifetime of loneliness, not because I won't have children who will look after me when I'm old, but because my lifestyle choices will never be approved, or accepted, by my elders and, perhaps, quite possibly, my peers (I know I shouldn't care what mere *peers* think when my actual friends love me unconditionally, but there you go). What happens when I find another partner, and together we build a home and a life, but never a portrait-ready nuclear family? What happens when my best friends, whom I see at least once a week at *this* specific point in our lives, become parents one day, and we cannot ever bridge that specific gap in our shared interests? I'm not an insecure thirteen-year-old anymore, but I still don't want to spend a lifetime eating lunch alone in a metaphorical toilet stall.

I was taught that family and familial loyalty are everything, and that you cannot turn your back on someone with whom you are bound by blood; growing up, I held on to these beliefs, tightly and consistently. The idea of a "chosen family" seems absurd in this context—the wonderfully frustrating thing about family is that you don't get to choose them, right?

My breakup was one of the hardest things I'd ever gone through. "I'm going to be alone! I'm so *old*! How am I going to go on a first date again? I'm going to die alone! You're all going to be old and get married! And what will I be?" I lamented the next day as I sobbed into a burrito at Khin's house.

"Alone?" Khin ventured, smirking.

"ALONE!" I yelled back, and sobbed some more.

Khin didn't flinch, and with near-complete disinterest, said with a roll of her eyes, "You're not going to die alone. You have us!"

I got my first period when I was eight. I had the worst stomach cramps in the months preceding it, and Mom took me to several different doctors, none of whom could come up with a diagnosis (no one thinks an eight-year-old is having premenstrual cramps); one afternoon, we were out shopping and the pain was the worst it'd ever been, and Mom thought she was going to have to rush me to the hospital until I ran into a bathroom and saw the blood. Unlike the rest of my friends, who got their periods around the same time several years later and could collude with one another if they needed an emergency pad in the middle of class, being an eight-year-old on her period was one of the most bizarre and isolating experiences of my life. I didn't tell any of my friends that

I'd gotten my period (to be honest, I didn't even really know what a period was yet) and that I was now, biologically speaking, a woman; I thought maybe they would laugh or think I was weird or not want to hang out with me anymore for being a freak. One day in the middle of recess, however, I went to the bathroom and found that my period had come, and too ashamed to ask a teacher or the school nurse for a pad, I had no other option but to confide in my girlfriends about what had happened. My friend Shoon located her older sister, told her that she needed a pad, and then a small group of us huddled together inside a toilet stall. "I don't know how to use it, my mom just puts it on for me," I sheepishly admitted (I'd only had a couple of cycles by this point). But Shoon opened and tore the pad off of its backing, told me not to worry because she'd seen her sister do this before (she had not), and then slapped the sticky bottom part of the pad onto my vulva. It is such a humiliating and funny story, but in retrospect, it's also just one of the nicest, most heartwarming things anyone's ever done for me. No one thought I was a freak for being on my period, no one got grossed out by the blood; all they knew was that I needed help and that they were going to help me to the best of their abilities, regardless of our collective ignorance about how menstrual products worked. And in those moments when I wonder how or if I'm going to find a community that accepts me for the kind of woman

I am (in this case, the kind that gets her period when she's eight), I remind myself that I already have that.

This started out as a piece exploring girlhood and womanhood, and specifically, what it means to be a Myanmar woman once you reject something that is thought of as so central to womanhood in this context. And then as I kept writing, it started asking questions of family and community, and of what happens when, as a person with a womb, you shirk your responsibilities of expanding said family and community, and what *that* means in the context of a culture that, as I've said, prides itself on being family-oriented. For what felt like ages, I tried to find some form of neat narrative arc that culminated in me now facing the world with a new, more informed, and more concrete definition of womanhood. But I don't have one. I don't quite know what it means when I say that I am a woman, not because I am unsure of it, but because I'm not quite certain what it means to be a woman in the first place.

Take, for example, the fact that women are seen as natural nurturers, right? For a long time, I fought against this label. I'd think, *What, just because I'm a woman, I'm supposed to have this innate ability to care for others? I don't know how to change a diaper, and I don't want to learn how to!* I didn't want to be a nurturing woman, or a woman who was seen as gentle and soft; because if I were those things, then that would just give everyone else more ammunition to convince me that I would one day become a good mother. But, I've learned, nurturing means different things. My friends who have killed many plants over the past several years (even the ones that the sellers ensured them required "practically no care") nurtured me through heartbreak. I care for Mom when she is sick. And, a lot of times, I nurture *myself* through illness, heartbreak, rejection, embarrassment, and getting ghosted by shitty dudes. I can be a woman who is good at taking care of those I love without ever wanting to take care of my own child—both of these things can be true. I can also be a woman who is comfortable being on my own but never wants to lose the love and support of my community, biological and chosen.

And if I get to redefine what it means to be a woman, and specifically a Myanmar woman, then surely I also get to redefine what I mean by *family* and *community*, along with the kinds of families and communities I am a part of. I don't want to be in a community where I am mandated to play a very specific role, and am vilified or mocked if I fail to show interest in doing so. That's not what a community should do. There's a scene in the show *The Bold Type* where one of the main characters gets a yoni egg stuck in her vagina, and while she lies on her back, one of her best friends kneels down and reaches in to retrieve it. "Just so you know, I would one hundred percent remove a yoni egg from any of your vaginas," Khin told me and Poe after we watched that episode; we have no doubt she means it, and *will* still mean it when we're eighty and if, for some reason, one of us has managed to get a yoni egg lodged inside our eighty-year-old crotch. I'm sure babies and parenthood are great, but speaking for myself, I kind of love being part of families, chosen as they may be, where we slap pads onto, or yank small jade eggs out of, one other's vaginas if and when we are summoned to do so (I ask you, "Would a baby do that?"). Maybe our mothers and grandmothers and aunties' communities struggle to accept women who do not want children. But communities adapt and evolve, hopefully into better iterations of themselves. We will make new communities that are better and more unconditional in their kindness and open-mindedness. We already have.

The other thing I remember about The Time I Ate My Lunch in a Toilet Stall is that after I'd shoved my now-empty Styrofoam container back into my bag, washed my hands, and stepped out into the lobby, I saw Poe standing by the main glass entrance doors and obviously scanning the halls for me. When we locked eyes, she waved and walked over, and, linking her arm in mine, said, "Where were you? I was looking for you."

MYANGLISH

The United States Foreign Service Institute divides languages into groups of difficulty for English-language speakers. Myanmar falls into Group 3, which means it's a "hard language" and demonstrates "significant linguistic and/or cultural differences from English," requiring approximately forty-four weeks of learning or 1,100 class hours. At the time of writing this, I've been learning Myanmar for over 1,200 weeks or 201,600 hours (and counting).

I was lucky enough to grow up in a bilingual household. As a result of her childhood and the fact that she spent most of her school years in foreign countries, Mom became fluent in English and French as well as Myanmar, while A May picked up enough English to get by during her time abroad. When I was born, right from the start, my mother and grandmother spoke to me in both English and Myanmar as much as possible, as though we were actually a bilingual family and it was imperative that I get as early of a head start on my English as my Myanmar. Even though A May wasn't fully fluent, she still taught me as best as she could, focusing on numbers and basic vocabulary. Mom still recalls how whenever we had guests over, A May would sit me down in front of them, along with a large bucket of zoo animal toys, and say, "Watch this." She'd take out one toy at a time, and I would identify each one in English: "Lion. Tiger. Zebra." The guests weren't allowed to get on with their business until the two of us had gone through the whole bucket. It was her favorite party trick, and she would beam at me as I got each one right, and I would smile proudly back: *Look. Look, အမေ. Look what I can do.*

Mom worked hard so she could afford to send me and my siblings to our expensive international school, mainly because we were taught almost exclusively in English there. Like other parents in "developing countries" (as friends from Indonesia and India and Malaysia later told me), my parents' greatest fear was that I wouldn't be fluent in that most international and revered of languages, and they bought me as many books and movies and music CDs as I wanted, all of them in English. They weren't fans of a lot of aspects of Western culture, but they knew that if I wanted to succeed academically and, later, professionally, I would need to tick this most basic Eurocentric checkbox. I grew up on *The Magic*

School Bus and Hilary Duff and Enid Blyton. When I started college in the United States, my American professors were all amazed at how fluent I was in English; in their minds, Myanmar was this mysterious, faraway land that, at that time, in 2011, had only just begun reintegrating itself into the international community. Growing up, I got to practice my English on a daily basis because our family was privileged enough to afford satellite TV, through which we could watch English-language shows, as well as go on holidays abroad, where I bought English-language books that were scarce back home. That being said, even in the 1980s and '90s, when all of Myanmar was essentially cut off from the rest of the world, English usage still seeped into people's day-to-day lives, even for those who had never been out of the country. For instance, one quirky fact about Myanmar that always shocks foreigners—and truly is still one of our biggest mysteries—is our collective love for the Irish pop group Westlife. No one knows how or why Westlife took over the nation, but to this day, even locals who don't speak English will probably be able to sing you at least one Westlife song. The most probable theory behind their widespread and enduring popularity seems to be that "the English is spoken clearly, the music is accessible, the melodies are attractive, and Westlife is uncontroversial." As a child, I blasted Westlife on the car stereo during our summer road trips to A May's small hometown of Taungoo. Speaking English was a symbol of class status—my siblings and I spoke English because we went to an international school, which my parents afforded; in contrast, the rest of A May's family, most of whom still lived in Taungoo, knew little more than basic greetings like "Hello" and "Thank you." They marveled at how flawlessly my siblings and I communicated in English. But my family and I were so focused on my acquiring a new language that we never stopped to think of what I was losing.

A friend once told me that her mom, an artist, always says, "Writing is a muscle. If you don't use it regularly, it'll get weak." In school, I hated my Myanmar language classes. All the best literature in the world was written in English, or if not, it was translated into English. People write *about* Myanmar, not *in* its language. I was convinced that if I wanted to be a writer (and I did, from a young age), then I only needed to focus on conquering the English-language world; if it came to it, someone else would translate my works into Myanmar. I didn't care if my Myanmar-language muscle atrophied at an alarming rate until it flatlined and died.

With friends, I switched between Myanmar and English in casual conversation, but when it came to texting or emailing or any other form of written communication, we'd either write in English or turn to "Myanglish," having decided that creating a new hybrid language was easier than learning a preexisting one. Myanglish is particularly useful when we want to text or comment or post something online in Myanmar, but don't know how to spell what we want to say, and so instead we transliterate the word from Myanmar to English; believe it or not, somehow this seemed—still seems in a lot of cases—much easier and simpler than just learning how to write in Myanmar. If we want to express embarrassment toward an unflattering photo that a friend has posted online, we comment "Shet sa yar gyi" instead of "That's so embarrassing"; isn't it weird, and maybe even hopeful, that in spite of our limited written Myanmar, something in our brains is conditioned to instinctually think "Shet sa yar gyi" instead of "That's so embarrassing"? It's not perfect and maybe not even ideal in the eyes of our elders, but we try. We're always trying. When we find ourselves in a situation where we have to write a formal letter in Myanmar, we turn to our parents and, conveniently forgetting any and all past tantrums of "I'm an adult, I don't need you!" we ask them to write the letter for us. The last time this happened, my friends and I were in our mid-twenties, and we laughed at how many degrees we had between us (degrees from reputable foreign universities, in fact), and yet we couldn't write a simple letter. "Ugh, I really need to learn how to write," we each murmured with a sarcastic chuckle, almost as though we felt the need to include that addendum, to announce to the world, "Don't worry, I haven't forgotten, I *will* learn again one day, I promise."

While Dad was in the army, Mom would take some combination of car and boat and foot to visit him. This was before we could each afford our own mobile phone, and because there was little to no cell signal in each of these places, Dad would send back letters with Mom for us. Knowing I wouldn't be able to read Myanmar, he would write to me in English, even though his grasp of the language was weak. Due to their military family lifestyle, my father's parents never really saw the point in their children learning English. But Dad started dating Mom and became embarrassed that he couldn't converse with many of her colleagues when he accompanied her to professional functions, so over time, he learned enough English to hold a conversation or slowly read a text. The letters he would write me were short, succinct single pages, each letter of each word traced carefully so as not to make a mistake, like a page from a kid's penmanship workbook. The grammar wasn't perfect, the sentiments conveyed weren't as emotionally complex as they would've been had he been able to write in his native tongue, but he wrote what he knew were the key phrases: "I am always thinking of you." "I miss you so much." "I love you."

In his essay "To Please a Shadow," Russian writer Joseph Brodsky claims, "When a writer resorts to a language other than his mother tongue, he does so either out of necessity, like Conrad, or because of burning ambition, like Nabokov, or for the sake of greater estrangement, like Beckett." Brodsky also goes on to say that his own decision to write in English was mainly to pay tribute to, and *please*, Auden, whom he considered the greatest writer of his time. In retrospect, I have to confess that I spent all those years perfecting my English so that I, too, could please others. I wanted to please my parents and A May, who were constantly in the background and whose validation I craved, and my favorite writers, all of whom were white. In spite of my own Brownness, I was so sure I could emulate their talent and success if I just became fully fluent in the same language as them.

Today, I can read fast enough to keep up with the Myanmar-subtitled Indian soap operas that A May watches five days a week. Before I moved out, this was our tradition: after dinner, from 8:00 to 8:30 p.m., Monday to Friday, A May and I sit down with our cups of tea—hers traditional Myanmar green, mine English breakfast—and watch *Gangaa*. I read the subtitles as quickly as I can, for fear that I might miss a joke or a dramatic reveal that we can randomly reference the next day to everyone else's ignorance, thus further strengthening our bond. At 8:31 p.m., I pat myself on the back for spending quality time with my grandmother, for being the only grandchild who can. *At least I'm not as bad as them*, I think, ignoring all the other ways in which I could still be better.

I don't quite remember when it was that I began feeling ashamed of my limited Myanmar. I recall one afternoon, when I was in fourth or fifth grade, Mom's friend stopped me outside of school and asked me how to spell Dad's name for a wedding invitation. I furrowed my brow and tried my hardest to recall what his name looked like on forms, but after about twenty seconds of silence, the auntie smiled and said, "You know what? It's okay, I'm sure I've spelled it correctly." I never viewed learning my native tongue as a necessity, and it never was—my parents would fill out forms for me, and apart from the one Myanmar-language class that I absolutely hated, all of my homework was done in English. In *After Babel*, George Steiner argues that different groups of humans developed their own languages as a means to maintain privacy, to "conceal and internalize more, perhaps, than they convey outwardly." The more I lost Myanmar and gained English, the more the divide between myself and my parents and grandparents solidified. As a teenager who wanted privacy more than anything in the world, I didn't mind this chasm; I didn't mind that A May or Dad could never fully understand what I was saying to my friends when I talked on the phone right in front of them—in fact, I liked it. Once I moved to the United

States to start college, I had more or less decided that I was never going to (re)learn Myanmar because I would never again have any use for it.

I got my first real boyfriend a few months after the start of my freshman year—let's call him M. M was a year above me, and he loved everything to do with geography and history and languages. He took German as his language elective and practiced with friends from class whenever he saw them at lunch or in the evening. He was also a very proud Polish American, and while I lowered my voice on the phone when I spoke in Myanmar to my family in public, M roamed campus loudly talking to his dad in Polish. Soon after we started dating, he asked me to teach him basic Myanmar. I taught him numbers, and then some vocabulary, and still he craved to learn more—I had never seen someone so voracious to learn Myanmar—so I taught him basic grammar. There was one other Myanmar student on campus apart from me, and whenever M saw her, he would put together the few sentences that he could and she'd laugh and be impressed, and he'd grin: *Look what I can do.*

It was, quite simply, mind-boggling to me that this person who spoke English and Polish and German and Russian was this excited to learn a language that I actively hated. I was taking French classes at the same time, but M never asked me to teach him any French.

"I'm just not interested," he'd say.

But what about Flaubert? I'd wonder. *Or Hugo, or Camus, or Sand?* At the time, I was fascinated with French literature, not to mention also a little infatuated with the idea of becoming fluent in a *romance* language, and I viewed French as one of the most important and esteemed of literary languages. But M didn't. He thought it was overrated and boring. He didn't care about counting from un to dix, but he wanted to learn how to write all the Myanmar numbers, from ၁ to ၁၀. We were together for two and a half years. He was my first for a lot of things, including the first person to make me actually, truly, curiously excited about learning Myanmar. I loved him, and he loved when I would teach him how to write and speak Myanmar, and so I started loving our lessons too.

One of my literature professors in college was always fascinated by the concept of liminality; I didn't know what it meant at first, but when I found out, I instantly recognized it as the place that I'd been occupying my whole life. When first-generation or second-generation Asian immigrant friends confess that they're ashamed that they can't communicate with family members back home in their native language, I am again smug and think, *That could never be me. Imagine not being able to talk to A May about my day!* but I'm sure on more than one occasion, someone else who has a higher level of fluency than me has thought the same of me. The Myanmar language isn't foreign to me—I talk to my grandma in it every day, I read road signs and news articles and memes in Myanmar—but I don't know it as wholly and effortlessly as I'd like to, as I should. I'm not able to quickly scan a document and note the key points. I couldn't read you two-thirds of the alphabet if you showed me all the letters on a poster, but if you showed me a word, I could probably use phonetics to figure out how it sounded. It's a similarly strange and puzzling problem when it comes to writing, as well, because my hand still knows how to spell sounds, but because there are multiple ways to spell different sounds, my brain doesn't know which spellings go together to form a specific word; it can write phonetically, but it gets lost when two or more groups of letters make the same sound. For example, to make a comparison in English, I know how *brain* sounds, and I know how to write both "ain" and "ane" and the fact that they both sound the same, but I don't know if *brain* is spelled "brain" or "brane"; when I refer to the act of using my teeth to cut into something to eat, do I spell it "bite" or "byte"?

A May is told by my mom and teachers that I am a brilliant writer, and she believes it in the way grandparents always believe their grandchildren are brilliant at everything they do, but she's never been able to really see it for herself. For my undergraduate thesis, I wrote over a hundred pages on literary realism in nineteenth-century

European literature; my parents insisted on having a bound copy themselves, and now, six years later, it still sits in the middle of our living room coffee table, telling every visitor who sits down: *Look what our daughter can do.* A May was one of the first people I mentioned and thanked in my acknowledgments, and yet I know that she will never be able to understand more than a paragraph of the work, if that. I want to write something, anything—a poem, an essay, a short story, a novel—in my mother tongue, in her tongue, and show it to her: *Look. Look,* အမေ. *Look what I can do.*

Before she became a full-time stay-at-home mom, A May was a math teacher, and every school year she would teach me from my math textbooks, proud—and maybe, grateful—that she was an expert in the one subject that didn't require her to know much English. Mom helped me with science and social studies and French, but numbers were A May's domain—that is, until I got to high school and I started taking higher-level classes where the math went beyond just numbers and involved English words and concepts. She held up her hands in defeat when she could no longer understand what the problems in the textbook and the answers in my notebook said, when they were no longer written in just the language of numbers but also relied on a fluency in English. I started doing my math homework on my own, and I hated it—I missed A May, I missed being able to speak the same language as her.

When I was a teenager, I found one of Dad's letters in the drawer of my work table many years after I had first received it. Reading it again, I felt an urge to go back in time and ask him to tell me more. I wanted to know what he did every day, how often he thought about me, what plans he had for us the next time he came home; the chasm, the privacy between us that I had craved at the time, was now something I despised, and I longed for my father to have been able to "convey outwardly," as Steiner put it, all the things that language was cutting off and concealing between us.

I had a pact with myself not to write this essay until I could write it in both English and Myanmar, but now I don't see when or even *if* that will ever happen. It always comes back to the writing. I attended a summer writing camp when I was fourteen, and halfway through my three weeks there, I knew that this was what I wanted to do for a living; no other side hobby or subject in school was ever again up for consideration. After I graduated, it took me several years to start telling people that I was a writer; I held a full-time journalism role for less than a year and referred to myself as a freelance journalist for a while afterward, but it never felt entirely accurate. I thought it was obnoxious of me to label my own job as that of "writer," as though it was a title that I could only have bestowed upon me by other people. But this is what I do. I am a writer, I have two degrees in Creative Writing—capital *C*, capital *W*; but these degrees are in English, and I have to use Google Translate to text my aunt. I need to check with my mother or grandmother on how to spell my sister's name. When A May took me to the bank to open a new bank account, I had to fill out a form in Myanmar, and the bank employee was puzzled as to why it was taking me so long to spell my address and why my grandmother ended up having to fill it out for me. On my CV, I state that I am fully fluent in reading, writing, and speaking in English, and fully fluent in reading and speaking in Myanmar, and every time I apply for a new job, I quietly hope that they won't notice the omission. People want to know how someone who gets paid to write doesn't know how to write in their native language. I get embarrassed because I don't have a good answer. Trust me, I want to know too.

My first ever published article when I started out as a journalist was an op-ed titled "Could I see the Myanmar menu, please?" I wrote it after a family dinner at a new restaurant where the menu was entirely in English; we had gone with several members of my extended family from A May's side, but Mom and I were the only ones fluent in English, and so my embarrassed relatives left it to us to order for them, ashamed to ask the server what each dish meant in Myanmar. The experience left me furious on their behalf, and I pitched and sold the piece a few weeks later. In it, I wrote:

> I'm tired of going out to dinner with Myanmar friends who are perfectly well-educated but have no idea how to read the menu and are reduced to pointing at pictures or asking the waiter. It's embarrassing.

> I'm all for restaurants and chefs sharing other nation's foods with our country, but you cannot share much, if at all, if you are adamant about sticking to a foreign language. That's not sharing with the Myanmar people; that's sharing with a select few who speak English.

The piece garnered a bit of buzz, and one of the restaurants I interviewed even rolled out a Myanmar-language menu shortly afterward. I was proud of myself. However, as I was collecting quotes from all of those restaurants, a small voice in my mind kept whispering that I was a hypocrite, a phony. One manager I interviewed defended the restaurant's choice by saying that their brand is "international," and that "English is the most common language"—defenses that were so painfully similar to the ones *I* had given over the years when asked why I never learned how to write in Myanmar. Another voice that took even more effort to ignore pointed out how much more impactful this article would be if I could've also written it in Myanmar so that the very people I was standing up for could read my words.

Not all languages are created equal. "One language dies every 14 days," according to a 2012 *National Geographic* article, which also estimates that only approximately half of the preexisting seven thousand or so languages will still be alive in the twenty-second century, the dead ones having been replaced by English, Mandarin, or Spanish. This is heartbreaking, but not unprecedented—230 languages became extinct between 1950 and 2010.

Maybe one day I will learn to write Myanmar again—not Myanglish, but real Myanmar, with the actual curly Myanmar script—from scratch, using workbooks designed for kindergarteners. Still, sometimes I wonder if maybe I wouldn't care as much about all of this if my day-to-day livelihood and identity as an artist did not rely entirely on my mastery of the written word; perhaps if I were a photographer or a painter, this would be less of a constant concern, and feel like less of an innate shortcoming on my part. There is a fear that I am either less of a writer or less Myanmar because I cannot combine the two; I am still working through this, and in the process, reminding myself that just because I cannot write in the Myanmar language does not mean that I am not a Myanmar writer. That being said, I know that my written Myanmar will never be as good as my written English; I have made my peace with this; a muscle that you only really start using in your late twenties cannot ever be as strong as one you've been using since birth.

But, I tell myself, it still says something that even after all of this time, I still try, I *am* still trying. Dad's letters meant as much as they did, and in spite of their spelling mistakes and imperfect grammar, because I could see how much effort he'd put into them. And when, and as difficult as it can be sometimes, I'm able to put my writer's ego aside, it hits me that it is not the physical act of writing that gives words and language weight and meaning; a grandiose speech through which someone vulnerably and openly declares their love is just as poignant as the most romantic of love letters. I always think it's sweet that whenever I ask couple friends of mine with different native languages, "So can you say anything in X *language* yet?" they almost always blush and say, "Well, I know how to say 'I love you.'" After all, in the end, and as Dad's letters always remind me, whether I'm speaking or writing, and regardless of the language and my level of fluency, all I really need to know are the key phrases: "A myae tan thadi ya nay tae." "A yan lwan tae." "Chit tae."

Acknowledgments

When I got my book deal, writing the acknowledgments section was at the top of the list of things I was most looking forward to doing. To every person mentioned here, in the words of the inimitable Moira Rose: Aren't you a wolf pack by which any gal would be so lucky to be protected? (You are.)

Hayley Steed, my agent, who changed my life and cheered me on as I wrote this book during the most bizarre year and a half, who responds to my "What if this worst-case scenario comes true?!" emails with kindness and a game plan—thank you for, well, *everything*. I will never stop telling every writer to make sure they have a Hayley in their corner. All of my gratitude, always, to everyone at the Madeleine Milburn Literary, TV & Film Agency.

I used to say that my dream was to publish *a* book, but it wasn't until I started writing this book that I realized my dream was to publish *this* specific book. Thank you to my editor, Megha Majumdar, for wholeheartedly championing *this* book from the first read, for your invaluable editorial guidance, and for repeatedly reminding me to pause and be proud of my accomplishments. There's a lot of vague talk about how it's important for an editor to "get" a book and its author, but as soon as we had our very first call, I knew in my gut that Megha *got* it; what an honor to have one of my favorite writers become my editor and friend. Thank you, Nicole Caputo, Jaya Miceli, Wah-Ming Chang, Olenka Burgess, tracy danes, Laura Berry, Megan Low, Kendall Storey, Alisha Gorder, Megan Fishmann, Rachel Fershleiser, Alyson Forbes, Katie Boland, Laura Gonzalez, Dustin Kurtz, and everyone else at Catapult who helped make this book the very best it could be. Thank you for taking a chance on this baby debut author who used to think that getting a book published was the stuff of daydreams.

I like to say that I've technically been working on this book since 2013 when I wrote the opening chapter's very first draft for one of Jamie Hutchinson's classes. Jamie, thank you for being a mentor in life and literature. I'm sorry I've continued knocking on your door with new crises long after you stopped being contractually obliged to listen to me, but thank you for still doing so.

Thank you to my UEA Non-Fiction cohort who read the first drafts of several of these essays. Lucky, lucky me to be part of such a warm band of writers and friends.

In particular, thank you: Cailey Rizzo, hypewoman extraordinaire. Katie Simon, who excitedly talked me through even the most tedious parts of this whole journey. Marina Mahathir, who continuously inspires me and reminds me of the importance of our voices.

Thank you to every Myanmar woman writer who paved the way for my generation. I can't wait to see what we all continue to do. Thank you, especially, to MiMi Aye and Thirii Myo Kyaw Myint, for being so generous with their time and friendship.

I seem to be supremely talented at surrounding myself with the most supportive village, so thank you to all of you who listened to me moan about this book nonstop and was rooting for me before there was even a book deal on the table: Shaun Jacques, for supporting me wholeheartedly in anything and everything I've ever wanted to do, including leaving the house at 3:00 a.m. for a 9:00 a.m. flight; I love you and I like you, always. Hibba Mazhary, for a friendship built on Taylor Swift conspiracy theories and late-night Hassan's trips, and for whom I would eat all the ginger cookies in the world. Noah Quinn Shenker, who, during a freshman year lecture, glanced over at an essay idea I had begun drafting and then looked up at me and said, "You know, you're a really good writer"—thank you for believing in me even before day one, and for all our deep heart-to-hearts about IP. Rachel Wang, for making the longest twenty-four hours of our lives semibearable (let's literally never do that again!). Judith and U Ba Win, for always making sure I was well fed and not (too) homesick while I began carving out my own space in the world. Bernie Rodgers, for pushing me to become a more critical and overall *better* reader and writer, and for introducing me to some of my (now our!) favorite books and authors. Christian Brown, for the photos and for always putting up with our shenanigans. Mark, Sharon, Martin, and the rest of the Jacques and Moran families, for welcoming me in and loving me in spite of all the sass.

Thank you to my flesh and blood, who kind of just nodded along and believed me when I told them I was working on a book. Thank you to all my cousins and aunties and uncles for loving me across lifetimes and geographical borders. A May, for always making sure my stomach and brain were full. Pho Pho Tun, for passing on your love of reading. Phyo and Shan, for loving me and all my nerdiness despite being the coolest kids in the world. And my parents, for your endless patience and indomitable love, and for always being there for me whenever I told you I needed you. Mom, my pal who makes life the most fun, when it comes to you, the list goes on forever. You always say you love me more, but I love you most.

I read somewhere that the last acknowledgment is usually saved for the author's partner, so lastly, thank you to Khin Hnin Su and Poe Yu Hlaing, my forever partners in crime and celebration. Thank you for letting me take so many rain checks whenever I was in the middle of an editing storm, for being the sturdiest bitch bucket, and for helping me birth this book baby. I'll only publicly say this once, but you'll have it in writing forever: I love you.

Bibliography

A Me by Any Other Name

Daw Mi Mi Khaing, "Burmese Names," *Atlantic*, February 1958.

Gustaaf Houtman, *Mental Culture in Burmese Crisis Politics: Aung San Suu Kyi and the National League for Democracy* (Tokyo: Institute for the Study of Languages and Cultures of Asia and Africa, 1999).

Jonathan Soroff, "The Eyes Have It," *Improper Bostonian*, May 23, 2014.

Julio Cortázar, *Hopscotch: A Novel*, trans. Gregory Rabassa (New York: Pantheon Books, 1987).

Maung Thet Pyin, "Behind the Names of Streets, Roads in Downtown Yangon," *Myanmar Times*, September 18, 2018.

"Should It Be Burma or Myanmar?" BBC News, September 26, 2007.

Laundry Load

Daw Mya Sein, "The Women of Burma," *Atlantic*, February 1958.

Eve Ensler, *The Vagina Monologues*, (New York: Villard, 2007).

Lae Phyu Pya Myo Myint, "Artist Htein Lin Takes Aim at a Men's Custom," *Myanmar Times*, May 17, 2019.

"Myanmar Times Apologizes for Featuring 'Vagina Snack' in Food Article," *Coconuts Yangon*, October 19, 2015.

"Woman Arrested for Sarong Jibe," *Democratic Voice of Burma*, October 14, 2015.

Swimming Lessons

Anna Borges, "I Am Not Always Very Attached to Being Alive," *Outline*, April 2, 2019.

"Better Suicide Prevention and Mental Health Care Needed Among Myanmar's Most Vulnerable," United Nations Population Fund, March 4, 2020.

Koko Nishi, "Mental Health Among Asian-Americans," American Psychological Association, 2012.

A Baking Essay I Need to Write

Alexis Watts, "I've Never Felt Truly Mexican, But Cooking with My Mom Helps," *Bon Appétit*, January 31, 2019.

Brigid Washington, "This Simple, Soulful Dish Tells

the Story of My Ancestors," *Bon Appétit*, March 8, 2021.

Brigitte Malivert, "Layers of Obstruction," *Eater*, December 16, 2020.

Cory Baldwin, "How the KitchenAid Stand Mixer Achieved Icon Status," *Eater*, February 24, 2020.

Geeta Kothari, "If You Are What You Eat, Then What Am I?" *Kenyon Review* 21, no. 1 (Winter 1999): 6–14.

Jaya Saxena, "The Limits of the Lunchbox Moment," *Eater*, February 8, 2021.

MiMi Aye, *Mandalay: Recipes and Tales from a Burmese Kitchen* (London: Bloomsbury Absolute, 2019).

Unique Selling Point

Richard Jean So and Gus Wezerek, "Just How White Is the Book Industry?" *New York Times*, December 11, 2020.

Sarah Park Dahlen and David Huyck, "Diversity in Children's Books 2018," *Sarah Park Blog*, June 19, 2019.

Htamin sar chin tae

Aye Min Thant, "What I Saw During Myanmar's Coup," *New York Times*, February 2, 2021.

Tongue Twisters

Andrea Romano, "These Accents Are Considered Most

'Friendly' and 'Assertive' Abroad—Here's Where Americans Rank," *Travel + Leisure*, January 18, 2020.

Ben Rhodes, "What Happened to Aung San Suu Kyi?" *Atlantic*, September 26, 2019.

Bill Gardner, "From 'Shrill' Housewife to Downing Street: The Changing Voice of Margaret Thatcher," *Telegraph*, November 25, 2014.

Bob Secter, "Illinois Fights Back with Fluency Law: Foreign Teachers Create Language Gap in Colleges," *Los Angeles Times*, September 27, 1987.

Connie Guglielmo, "Black Panther Rules Marvel's World. Literally," CNET, August 29, 2020.

Donald L. Rubin, "Nonlanguage Factors Affecting Undergraduates' Judgments of Nonnative English-Speaking Teaching Assistants," *Research in Higher Education* 33, no. 4 (August 1992): 511–31.

Drew Harwell, "The Accent Gap," *Washington Post*, July 19, 2018.

James Lane, "The 10 Most Spoken Languages in the World," *Babbel Magazine*, June 2, 2021.

Mari J. Matsuda, "Voices of America: Accent, Antidiscrimination Law, and a Jurisprudence for the Last Reconstruction," *Yale Law Journal* 100, no. 5 (1991): 1329–407.

Michele Debczak, "Can You Ever Truly Lose Your Accent?" *Mental Floss*, January 21, 2020.

Michelle Tauber, "Priyanka Chopra on Being Told by Hollywood to Amp Up Her Indian Accent: 'This *Is* My Indian Accent!'" *People*, May 19, 2017.

"Michelle Yeoh: Portraying an Icon in 'The Lady,'" NPR, April 28, 2012.

Rachael Sigee, "Are Authentic Accents Important in Film and TV?" BBC Culture, January 16, 2020.

Sanyukta Iyer, "Priyanka Chopra: Everybody Thinks I Have a Fake Accent," *Times of India*, May 28, 2015.

Sara Harrison, "Five Years of Tech Diversity Reports—and Little Progress," *Wired*, October 1, 2019.

Scott Feinberg, "'Awards Chatter' Podcast—Chadwick Boseman ('Black Panther')," *Hollywood Reporter*, August 29, 2018.

Sheridan Prasso, "Meeting Aung San Suu Kyi Was Worth Getting Blacklisted For," *Bloomberg*, November 12, 2015.

Simon Hoggart, "Aung San Suu Kyi in Westminster: A Historic Occasion with Lots of Pachelbel," *Guardian*, June 22, 2012.

State of Illinois 84th General Assembly House of Representatives Floor Debate Transcription, Illinois General Assembly.

Paperwork

"Burma: Reject Discriminatory Marriage Bill," Human Rights Watch, July 9, 2015.

good, Myanmar, girl

Ira Byock, *The Best Care Possible: A Physician's Quest to Transform Care Through the End of Life* (New York: Avery Publishing, 2013).

Myanglish

George Steiner, *After Babel: Aspects of Language and Translation*, 3rd ed. (Oxford University Press, 1998).

Jacob Goldberg, "Why is Westlife So Popular in Myanmar?" *Coconuts Yangon*, June 21, 2018.

Joseph Brodsky, *Less Than One: Selected Essays* (New York: Farrar, Straus and Giroux, 2020).

Russ Rymer, "Vanishing Voices," *National Geographic*, July 2012.

"UNESCO Atlas of the World's Languages in Danger," UNESCO, 2010.

© Christian Brown

PYAE MOE THET WAR is a writer and digital media editor who was born and raised in Yangon, Myanmar. She received a BA from Bard College at Simon's Rock and MAs from University College London and the University of East Anglia, before moving back to Yangon, where she currently lives with her dogs. *You've Changed* is her debut book.